PRINCETON THEOLOGICAL MONOGRAPH

Series

D1500108

Dikran Y. Hadidian
General Editor

2

R. S. THOMAS: POET OF THE HIDDEN GOD

Meaning and Mediation
In the Poetry of R. S. Thomas

R. S. THOMAS: POET OF THE HIDDEN GOD

Meaning and Mediation in the Poetry of R. S. Thomas

Dewi Zephaniah

D. Z. Phillips

PICKWICK PUBLICATIONS
Allison Park, Pennsylvania

Published in the USA in 1986 by
PICKWICK PUBLICATIONS
4137 Timberlane Drive
Allison Park, PA 15101

Printed in Hong Kong

Library of Congress Cataloging-in-Publication Data
Phillips, D. Z. (Dewi Zephaniah)
    R. S. Thomas: poet of the hidden God.
    (Princeton theological monograph series; 2)
    Bibliography: p.
    Includes index.
    1. Thomas, R. S. (Ronald Stuart), 1913-   – Religion.
2. God in literature.   3. Religious poetry, English – History and
criticism.   4. Philosophy and religion in literature.   I. Title
II. Series.
PR6039.H618Z82   1986   821'.914   85-31998
ISBN 0-915138-83-2

To
R. S. Thomas and Will Roberts

Vere tu es Deus absconditus.

(Isaiah 45:15)

God can only be present in creation under the form of absence.

'He will laugh at the trials of the innocent.' Silence of God. The noises here below imitate this silence. They mean nothing.

It is when from the innermost depths of our being we need a sound which does mean something – when we cry out for an answer and it is not given us – it is then that we touch the silence of God.

As a rule our imagination puts words into the sounds in the same way as we idly play at making out shapes in wreaths of smoke; but when we are too exhausted, when we no longer have the courage to play, then we must have real words. We cry out for them. The cry tears out our very entrails. All we get is silence.

After having gone through that, some begin to talk to themselves like madmen. Whatever they may do afterwards, we must have nothing but pity for them. The others, and they are not numerous, give their whole heart to silence.

(Simone Weil)

'You believe then?' The poems are witness.

(R. S. Thomas)

Contents

Preface

This essay is offered as one philosopher's response to the poetry of R. S. Thomas. I am deeply grateful to R. S. Thomas for his generous permission to quote from his poetry in this essay. In the letter he wrote me on this occasion the poet observes, 'The tendency of a philosopher is to extract the ideas for inspection' and, with good reason, he is wary of such responses. In discussing the poet's ideas, I hope to have done justice to them in their poetic contexts. As a philosopher, however, I was struck by the similarity between the hard-won celebration of the sense of a hidden God, a *Deus absconditus*, in the poet's work, and the attempts of some of us in contemporary philosophy of religion to let the possibilities of religious belief come in at the right place.

The initial challenge to the poet's desire to mediate a religious sense comes from his figure of a peasant who suffers a life of unrelenting toil. In exploring his own reactions to the challenge, R. S. Thomas says in his letter that he has been 'trying to operate on as many levels as possible, mostly failing, being self-contradictory, open to refutation on the charge of inconsistency, but occasionally perhaps setting up overtones'. No doubt he imagines charges of inconsistency and contradiction being made by philosophers. But may it not be the case that the fault lies in the philosopher's desire to tidy things up; his refusal to recognise, with Wittgenstein, 'that what is ragged must be left ragged'? Religious belief can come in at the right place only if its essential precariousness is recognised; only if we see how a shift of aspect makes a world of difference. R. S. Thomas says in his letter, 'All is ambivalence, multivalence even. The same natural background, which, from one standpoint has facilitated my belief in God, has from another raised enormous problems.' There can be no serious poetry or philosophy concerning religion today where the possibility of such a shift of aspect is not recognised.

Standing in the way of such recognition is a major obstacle

which R. S. Thomas and I recognise. In his letter, writing of his many-sided response in the struggle to mediate a religious sense in verse, R. S. Thomas says, 'A principal feature, of which you are aware, is the revolt against a comfortable, conventional, simplistic view of God, mainly due to my non-academic background and the kind of parishes I have ministered in.' Whether the poet's background is non-academic is surely open to dispute, but, again, how ironic it is to find that, to a large extent, in contemporary philosophy of religion, the comfortable simplistic God turns out to be the creation of the 'academic' world. This does not mean that there is no genuine task for philosophy to perform, but it must be prepared to wait on the parishes as the poet has done. The resulting story, poetic or philosophical, will be a mixed one; but at least it will be real. What R. S. Thomas has given me is an opportunity to wait on work which has that quality of real faith and struggle.

I have been captivated, for many years now, by the paintings of Will Roberts, who has designed the jacket for this book. In them, the figure of the farmer looms large. In the paintings, as in the poetry of R. S. Thomas, there are internal relations between the labours of the farmer and the Temptation and Passion of Christ. It was my good fortune to find Will Roberts glad to be associated with my essay. I should like to think that this particular convergence of interest in a poet, painter and philosopher is indicative of a wider convergence of interest in deep questions which keep recurring in these disciplines. For my part, I am honoured to dedicate this essay to two artists who, in different ways, wrestle with the mediation of religious sense in their respective spheres.

In the preparation of the typescript of the essay I benefited, as usual, from the excellent services of Mrs Valerie Gabe, Secretary to the Department of Philosophy. I am also grateful for the excellent editorial services of Mrs Valery Rose, and for the readiness of Dr Donald Evans in helping me with the proofreading.

Swansea   D. Z. PHILLIPS

Acknowledgements

The author and publishers wish to thank the following who have kindly given permission for the use of copyright-material:

The British Broadcasting Corporation for the extracts from *R. S. Thomas: Priest and Poet*, a transcript of the film for BBC Television, 2 April 1972, published in *Poetry Wales*, Spring 1972;

Granada Publishing Ltd for the extracts from *Song at the Year's Turning: Poems 1942–1954*, Rupert Hart-Davis, 1955; *Poetry for Supper*, Rupert Hart-Davis, 1958; *Tares*, Rupert Hart-Davis, 1961; *The Bread of Truth*, Rupert Hart-Davis, 1963; *Pietà*, Rupert Hart-Davis, 1966; *Not that he Brought Flowers*, Rupert Hart-Davis, 1968; and *Selected Poems 1946-1968*, Rupert Hart-Davis, 1973, all by R. S. Thomas;

Penguin Books Ltd for the extracts from *The Penguin Book of Religious Verse*, edited by R. S. Thomas, copyright © R. S. Thomas 1963; reprinted by permission of Penguin Books Ltd;

Poetry Wales Press for the extracts from *R. S. Thomas: Selected Prose*, edited by Sandra Anstey, Introduction by Ned Thomas, 1983;

Every effort has been made to trace all the copyright-holders but if any have been inadvertently overlooked the publishers will be pleased to make the necessary arrangement at the first opportunity.

Introduction

Many philosophers view appeals to literature with suspicion. A corresponding suspicion of philosophers when they do appeal to literature is felt by students of literature. The latter feel, often with good reason, that works of literature are simply being used by philosophers as examples of some general thesis; their intrinsic nature and qualities being seen as subservient to a wider enterprise. Yet, the philosophical appeal to literature need not have these consequences. The appeal can use what is shown in literature as a reminder of what the tendency to generalise in philosophy is tempted to ignore. It is this craving for generality, the desire to determine *the* logic of this or that area of discourse, which has led philosophers to view the use of literature in their subject with suspicion. The complexity found in literature, a complexity which characterises all serious aspects of human activity, can be seen as an irritating obstacle to arriving at the simple, pure, logical form of these activities. If we think that moral endeavour of various kinds, for example, can be reduced to a simple model, the complexities embodied in literature will be seen as marginal features incidental to the central issues philosophers wish to raise. Waiting on literature shows, however, that such complexities are internally related to and inextricably bound up with what can and cannot be said of moral considerations in a variety of contexts.[1]

Philosophers, of course, often raise questions, quite properly, which need not be the immediate concern of a work of literature. I refer to the traditional questions of aesthetics concerning such issues as the relation of fact and fiction, what is involved in reading a text, what is meant by an author's intentions, etc., etc. I am not suggesting that these issues cannot preoccupy a literary artist; they can and do. All I am saying is that there are conceptual issues concerning literature which concern the philosopher. But I am also saying that these questions will not be advanced very far without waiting on literature.

My emphasis in the present essay is slightly different. It would be artificial in the extreme so to compartmentalise culture that all overlaps between philosophy and literature are denied. When certain aspects of human activity come to be questioned in a radical way, it is not surprising to find that questioning taking different forms in different aspects of the culture. The questioning of the meaningfulness of religious belief is the most obvious example of what I have in mind. The way in which religion is subjected to criticism can characterise philosophical and literary preoccupations. It was such a parallel which led me to write an essay on five plays by a contemporary Welsh dramatist, Gwenlyn Parry.[2] The ways in which his characters are worried about the sense of what they are doing are embodiments of a story which begins with the positivistic attack on religion, progresses through the tensions of competitive secular self-reliance, and culminates in the re-emergence of pseudo-religion in the form of interest in the occult. The struggles he portrays, the thrust and counter-thrust of the plots, have remarkable parallels with the form argument has taken in the philosophy of religion in the second half of the twentieth century.

My preoccupation with the poetry of R. S. Thomas springs from a similar perspective. Here, too, I am fascinated by the struggle with sense, the struggle with the possibility of a satisfactory religious syntax in verse today. That struggle, unsurprisingly, shares many features of the philosophical thrusts and counter-thrusts which have characterised the discussion of religion in contemporary philosophy. Unlike the plays of Gwenlyn Parry, however, a sense emerges from the poetic struggle. In the plays, the emphasis is on religious meanings which cannot, for various reasons, withstand the assaults of criticism. Those defeats are emphasised in R. S. Thomas's poetry too, but there is also a hard-won celebration of a religious sense which survives the assaults.

It is this hard-won celebration that I missed in a previous article on the poetry of R. S. Thomas; an article which, as a result, did less than justice to his work. It is impossible to understand the poetic celebration to which I refer unless one appreciates the centrality for R. S. Thomas of the notion of a *Deus absconditus*, a hidden God. In the present essay, I hope to rectify my previous omission.

In the conclusion of my 1977 article, I reacted to the lines in 'Death of a Poet',

                        now he dies
            Intestate, having nothing to leave
            But a few songs, cold as stones
            In the thin hands that asked for bread.³
                            ('Death of a Poet')

by saying,

> We do not know whether R. S. Thomas would judge himself
> in this way. In any case there is a desirable asymmetry
> between first person and third person judgements in these
> matters. That is certainly not how we should see his poems.
> True, he has given us no entirely satisfactory religious syntax
> in verse. To what extent is such a syntax possible in the
> English language today? But, then, R. S. Thomas has ac-
> cepted no easy substitutes, no pat replies, and the integrity of
> his poetic voice is in the expression of our impotence where
> these matters are concerned. He also shows us those for whom
> such questions do not arise. He shows us the opportunists and
> the foreshorteners of eternity. He shows us those who endure
> with resignation, and he salutes them. Yet he does not turn
> from the larger questions of order and contingency, although
> he may think that in the end we have no longer any satisfac-
> tory answer to them. . . . Poetry breaks the thin window
> between R. S. Thomas and life, and we see how his mind cuts
> itself as it goes through.⁴

I have not changed my mind about the improbability of a
satisfactory religious sense in verse today. But that makes R. S.
Thomas's achievement all the more remarkable. We can ask,
with George Thomas, 'where else in the United Kingdom could
a modern poet write so simply within the context of the Bible
story even though his mind is attuned to, and subtly aware of,
the intricate problems that face the present-day interpretation of
Christianity?'⁵

   In 1967, in his Introduction to his selection from George
Herbert's verse, R. S. Thomas observes, 'Yeats said that out of
his quarrel with others, a man makes rhetoric, but out of his
quarrel with himself poetry. Herbert surely had no quarrel with
others. What he had was an argument, not with others, nor with

himself primarily, but with God; and God always won.'[6] There will be plenty of evidence in the course of this essay of the quarrels which engage R. S. Thomas. There is no denying the continuity between his preoccupations and Herbert's. R. S. Thomas says that Herbert demonstrates 'both the possibility and the desirability of a friendship with God. Friendship is no longer the right way to describe it. The word now is dialogue, encounter, confrontation; but the realities engaged have not altered all that much.'[7] In 1975, 'R. S. Thomas gave a broadcast interview in which he stated that he had become obsessed by the possibility of having "conversations or linguistic confrontations with ultimate reality".'[8]

What does such a linguistic confrontation involve? In his Introduction to *The Penguin Book of Religious Verse* R. S. Thomas says of religious revelation,

> The need for revelation at all suggests an ultimate reality beyond human attainment, the *mysterium tremendum et fascinans*. And here, surely, is common ground between religion and poetry. But there is the question of the mystic. To him the *Deus absconditus* is immediate; to the poet He is mediated. The mystic fails to mediate God adequately insofar as he is not a poet. The poet, with possibly less immediacy of apprehension, shows his spiritual concern and his spiritual nature through the medium of language, the supreme symbol.[9]

R. S. Thomas has said of himself, 'I'm a solitary. I'm a nature mystic; and silence and slowness and bareness have always appealed.'[10] As a poet attracted by mysticism, R. S. Thomas is therefore, unsurprisingly, absorbed in the struggle of mediating the sense of a *Deus absconditus*, a hidden God, in language. This struggle, of course, is not confined to poetry. Any age is confronted with the question of how possible it is to mediate an authentic religious sense. Without such mediation, religious language becomes trivial or nonsensical. The sense which religion may have is threatened by a variety of factors, factors which may threaten the very substance of faith itself.

When the poet says that religious revelation implies 'an ultimate reality beyond human attainment' it is clear that he would want to concur with Simone Weil when she says,

8

There is a reality outside the world, that is to say, outside
space and time, outside man's mental universe, outside any
sphere whatsoever that is accessible to human faculties.

Corresponding to this reality at the centre of the human
heart, is the longing for an absolute good, a longing which is
always there and is never appeased by any object in this
world.[11]

R. S. Thomas knows full well, however, that such talk has
become problematic for us. Commenting on difficulties which
philosophers and others have raised, M. O'C. Drury says,

but suppose someone was to say to me, 'what in the world do
you mean, outside of space and time? The word "outside"
only has a meaning *within* the categories of space and time.'
. . . This is a perfectly logical objection, the words 'out-
side space and time' have no more meaning than Plato's
beautiful expression 'the other side of the sky'. Again if some-
one were to object, 'I don't feel any longing for an absolute
good which is never appeased by any object in this world',
how could you arouse such a desire? What right have you to
make the psychological assertion that such a desire lies at the
centre of the human heart. . . . Yet I believe that Simone Weil
is right when she goes on to say that we must never *assume* that
any man, whatsoever he may be, has been deprived of the
power of having the longing come to birth. But how can this
desire for the absolute good be aroused? Only, I believe, by
means of an indirect communication. By so limiting the sphere
of 'what can be said' that we create a feeling of spiritual
claustrophobia. The dialectic must work from the inside as it
were.[12]

The reader may well wonder how an expression which is called
beautiful is nevertheless said to have no meaning, or why it is
located beyond 'what can be said'. Such criticisms will concern
us later in the essay. What survives such criticisms is Drury's
insistence that religious sense is communicated indirectly, that
the dialectic must work from the inside. That this should be so is
not an optional strategy. On the contrary, it marks the context in
which religious concepts have their sense and application. Si-
mone Weil emphasises this conceptual point in a striking way:

'Earthly things are the criterion of spiritual things. . . . Only
spiritual things are of value, but only physical things have a
verifiable existence. Therefore the value of the former can only
be verified as an illumination projected on to the latter.'[13] The
necessity of such illumination as a condition of sense makes
problematic the mystic's claim to immediacy. R. S. Thomas has
said,

> One gets the impression of a general dissatisfaction with
> Christianity as too rarefied, too mythical, too unrelated to the
> world of flesh and blood. Yet it has been called the most
> material of the great religions. 'The Word was made flesh and
> dwelt among us.' 'I believe in the resurrection of the body.' Its
> concern with the minute particulars is obvious; in what other
> religion worthy of the name do flesh and blood, bread and
> wine, earth and water, beasts and flowers play so prominent
> and important a part?[14]

Whatever of these criticisms, the mediation of religious sense is
certainly beset by many obstacles and difficulties. A powerful
tradition in philosophy proceeds on the assumption that belief in
God entails a belief in an order and purpose in human affairs. If
this purpose and order were known, they would serve as justifi-
cations of how things are. In this tradition, some philosophers
attempt to justify God's ways to men. The presence of evil in the
world, for example, is justified in terms of a higher or eventual
good. All theodicies, in the end, depend on such an assumption.
R. S. Thomas's poems force us to ask whether such assumptions
are feasible, let alone seemly.

Not all philosophers who believe in the availability of ultimate
explanations and justifications seek to justify God's ways to men.
On the contrary, they may deny the availability of these justifi-
cations while man is on earth; their content is mysterious to us.
Some have argued that theism, traditionally conceived, depends
on mysteries born of irredeemable ignorance. Finite creatures
can never hope to understand an infinite God. Our language,
our modes of understanding, are inherently inadequate to talk of
a transcendent God. God is beyond conceptual truth. There are
indications that now and again R. S. Thomas has been in-
fluenced by this style of philosophical reflection.

Yet, it would be a mistake to assume that the influences on the poet are all of one kind. The attraction which mysticism has for him enables him to speak of religious mystery in a way very different from that already indicated. In his fascination with the notion of a *Deus absconditus*, the poet sees God's will as not being contingently mysterious to us, but as born of a sense of mystery. On this view, we are not hidden from God by an inherently inadequate language. On the contrary, the idea of God in the language is of a hidden God. Confused conceptions of God's presence have to be purged in order that the idea of God as a *Deus absconditus* may come in at the right place. The 'coming in at the right place' is what constitutes the mediation of the concept. Such is the desire for gods of other kinds that the mediation may well take the form of a purifying atheism. Struggle is seldom far away from religious faith. Faith is threatened by various forms of impatience, some comic, some sinister. Notable among these are attempts to take eternity by storm. The variety of the assaults on religion is found in R. S. Thomas's work. That is why the thrusts and counter-thrusts in his poetry cannot be ignored if we want to appreciate what is involved in one of the most central of his ideas, that of a *Deus absconditus*, a hidden God. Many commentators have called attention to the concept of a hidden God, but very rarely is an attempt made to bring out the philosophical and theological implications of the concept in any detail. The present essay is an effort to remedy this situation.

1 Gestures and Challenges

R. S. Thomas was ordained in the Church in Wales in 1937 and took up his first country living as Rector of Manafon in Montgomeryshire. It was there that he brought out *The Stones of the Field* (1946) and *An Acre of Land* (1952), two of the works to be collected later in *Song at the Year's Turning* (1955). As Moelwyn Merchant has argued, these works 'set the main lines of his creativity for the succeeding twenty years'.[1] But what do these main lines amount to? From the beginning, they have to do with the mediation of sense and, in particular, religious sense, in human life. As we have already seen, according to one powerful tradition in philosophy, such mediation depends on finding order and purpose in human life. We have no direct proof of God's existence, but we do have evidence of his existence in his works. We are surrounded by order and design. People have always found these assumptions problematic. The most powerful attack on them in philosophical literature is found in David Hume's *Dialogues Concerning Natural Religion*. We cannot infer more of God's character than the evidence allows and, with all the religious good will in the world, he seems to be at best capricious. Calling God 'good' by inference from what we see around us, seems to go beyond what the facts allow.

R. S. Thomas shares Hume's misgivings. He knows too much of the harshness of life to give ready assent to the optimism of an argument from or to design. That harshness is presented to us, in the poet's first volume of poetry, *The Stones of the Field*, in the way of life of the country peasant. In the poet's bewilderment about what to make of this life we see, at the same time, the poet's bewilderment about how religious utterances are to be mediated in such situations. R. S. Thomas tells us that, when he took up his living in Manafon, he 'was brought up hard against this community [Montgomeryshire] and I really began to learn what human nature, rural human nature was like. And I must say that I found nothing that I'd been told in theological college was

1

of any help at all in these circumstances.'[2] It could be added that much of the religious apologetic found in contemporary philosophy of religion would be equally useless. The poet's bewilderment in being confronted by the peasant is obvious:

> Who can tell his years, for the winds have stretched
> So tight the skin on the bare racks of bone
> That his face is smooth, inscrutable as stone?
> And when he wades in the brown bilge of earth
> Hour by hour, or stoops to pull
> The reluctant swedes, who can read the look
> In the colourless eye, as his back comes straight
> Like an old tree lightened of the snow's weight?
> Is there love there, or hope, or any thought
> For the frail form broken beneath his tread,
> And the sweet pregnancy that yields his bread?
>
> ('A Labourer')[3]

Despite this picture, the poet also asserts, 'The earth is patient; he is not lost' (p. 17). The problem, however, is to make explicit what saying this amounts to. The poet's adversary in the thrust and counter-thrust of his wrestlings with this issue is the peasant figure Iago Prytherch. In a letter written in March 1969 to Raymond Garlick, R. S. Thomas indicated the origin of Iago Prytherch:

> As you will see from the poem 'And Prytherch, then, was he a real man?' – I have never been quite sure about his existence – he's certainly dead now! The first poem I wrote about him – 'A Peasant' – certainly was written in the evening after visiting a 1,000 feet up farm in Manafon where I saw a labourer docking swedes in the cold, grey air of a November afternoon. I came later to refer to this particular farmer jestingly as Iago Prytherch.

Many commentators on the poems which feature Prytherch have commented on the ambivalence in the poet's relation to him. Here are the first lines in which we are introduced to him:

> Iago Prytherch his name, though, be it allowed,
> Just an ordinary man of the bald Welsh hills,
> Who pens a few sheep in a gap of cloud.

Docking mangels, chipping the green skin
From the yellow bones with a half-witted grin
Of satisfaction, or churning the crude earth
To a stiff sea of clods that glint in the wind –
So are his days spent, his spittled mirth
Rarer than the sun that cracks the cheeks
Of the gaunt sky perhaps once in a week.
And then at night see him fixed in his chair
Motionless, except when he leans to gob in the fire.
There is something frightening in the vacancy of his mind.

('The Peasant')

What does this 'frightening vacancy' consist in? At first we might
assume that it is found in the peasant's inability to give an
account of his own situation. No matter how terrible that situa-
tion might be, a certain distancing is achieved in the very act of
being able to describe it. That is not open to Prytherch. Yet,
should such inability be equated with a vacancy of the mind?
There are times when the poet seems to commit the fallacy of
thinking that in order for the mind not to be deemed vacant, it
must be consciously posing large questions. Whether the activi-
ties of the peasant make sense, however, does not depend on
such intellectual assumptions. The sense, or lack of it, may show
itself in the style of a man's life without any articulation in
thought. But that does not remove the difficulty with which the
poet is confronted, for what *does* Prytherch's life show about the
sense of it? Does it not show a man who has been numbed by the
harshness of his labours? Could not this be the vacancy of mind
that the poet finds frightening? There is some reason to believe
this, since the poem can in no way be taken as a celebration of
intellectual articulateness in contrast to the vacancy of the
peasant mind. On the contrary, the poet has no time for an
intellectual affectation which would turn away in disgust from
the peasant:

His clothes, sour with years of sweat
And animal contact, shock the refined,
But affected, sense with their stark naturalness.

The poet is not denying that poetic, theological or philosophical
reflections constitute a certain kind of refinement, but he is
aware of the constant danger of such refinement being invaded

by affectation. Yet, the challenge of the peasant does not depend on this possibility. The life which bewilders the poet has qualities of its own to offer; an endurance which the affected sense knows little of.

> Yet this is your prototype, who, season by season
> Against siege of rain and the wind's attrition,
> Preserves his stock, an impregnable fortress
> Not to be stormed even in death's confusion.
> Remember him, then, for he, too, is a winner of wars,
> Enduring like a tree under the curious stars.[4]

Moelwyn Merchant is correct when he says,

> There are, then, no simple antitheses in these poems. They would have great dramatic interest if such an antithesis – the instinctive pastoral compassion of the priest confronting an object of apparent disgust – were their mainspring. But there is in fact neither antithesis nor reconciliation of attitude; both reactions, of compassionate admiration and distaste, are held, irreconcilable, within the texture of the poem.

The value of these remarks, however, is modified too cosily when Moelwyn Merchant goes on to claim, 'if an attitude is to be defined here at all, it is of total acceptance, recording grace and shame within their lives, with understanding, neutral charity and compassion'.[5] Here, the reference to a 'total acceptance', governed by such virtues, destroys the very tensions to which Moelwyn Merchant wishes to direct our attention. If a form of acceptance emerges later, it is of a different kind, one which cannot be anticipated at this stage of the poet's writing. What we have here is a shifting spectrum of aspects which strikes the poet as he confronts the peasant, each aspect striking home in its own way and exacting its own price. It is in this context that the poet struggles to mediate a kind of sense.

It is tempting, but misleading, to think that the poet rests contented in a saluting of the peasant's endurance, celebrating him as a 'winner of wars'. We must remember that, if the peasant endures, he does so 'under the curious stars'. The relation between the enduring human and the celestial order is one of curiosity. There is no neat fit, no ready intelligibility.

Only curiosity. Notice how we have moved somewhat from Hume's philosophical legacy where the problem is how to infer any intelligible divine order on the basis of order in the world we know. But in the poem the problem is reversed. The problem is how to make sense of the contingency of human life. The stars look down with curiosity.

How is it possible to speak of the stars in this way? It is not a question of any kind of inference from human affairs. The stars simply appear with this aspect in a reaction to the contingency of human affairs. The stars are above us, and at certain times they have been seen to look down on us with an assurance of stability, expressions of an unchanging order. They do not speak like that in R. S. Thomas's poem. There, the stars blink in astonished curiosity at the burdens men have to endure; they too, it seems, can make little sense of this strange fate. The problem is one of mediation, but in *The Stones of the Field* the force and vitality of the poems come from the importance of recognising the challenge expressed there, rather than from any real progress in meeting it. Nevertheless, the challenge is created for the poet and the theologian by the peasant. They are warned not to ignore what the peasant can show, despite the obvious temptation to do so.

> Consider this man in the field beneath,
> Gaitered with mud, lost in his own breath,
> Without joy, without sorrow,
> Without children, without wife,
> Stumbling insensitively from furrow to furrow,
> A vague somnambulist; but hold your tears,
> For his name also is written in the Book of Life.
> ('Affinity')

Further, why should the intellectual feel superior to him? What could he tell the peasant which would bring sense to his life? Indeed, they may have an affinity in a common need for such sense, and it is by no means obvious that it is the peasant's situation which is the less likely to yield it.

> Ransack your brainbox, pull out the drawers
> That rot in your heart's dust, and what have you to give
> To enrich his spirit or the way he lives?

From the standpoint of education or caste or creed
Is there anything to show that your essential need
Is less than his, who has the world for church,
And stands bare-headed in the woods' wide porch
Morning and evening to hear God's choir
Scatter their praises? Don't be taken in
By stinking garments or an aimless grin;
He also is human, and the same small star,
That lights you homeward, has inflamed his mind
With the old hunger, born of his kind.

(p. 25)

An extreme example of the kind of peasant R. S. Thomas has in
mind is found in his depiction of Twm, a dunce at school, who is
glad to leave at the age of fourteen to help his father on the farm.

His work was play after the dull school, and hands,
Shamed by the pen's awkwardness, toyed with the fleece
Of ewe and wether; eyes found a new peace
Tracing the poems, which the rooks wrote in the sky.

('The Airy Tomb')

But, before we assent too readily to this romantic readjustment,
the poet tells us that Twm's father dies when he is nineteen.
Accustomed as he is to seeing birth and death in nature, his grief
is soon healed. His mother insists that she will not outlive her
husband by a year. He is too busy with the farm to pay much
attention to her: 'bumpkin blind / To the vain hysteria of a
woman's mind'. But her prediction comes to pass. Twm carries
on with his relentless daily routine. He never bothers to go to the
town to socialise with his neighbours. Young women try to
interest him, but have no response. He becomes a local joke
because of his solitude. The poet, however, challenges the reader
and accuses him too of wanting a romantic ending to this grim
tale.

folk cannot abide

The inscrutable riddle, posed by their own kin.
And you, hypocrite reader, at ease in your chair,
Do not mock their conduct, for are you not also weary
Of this odd tale, preferring the usual climax?

The poet insists that the facts must be faced unadorned:

> No, no, you must face the fact
> Of his long life alone in that crumbling house
> With winds rending the joints, and the grey rain's claws
> Sharp in the thatch . . . .

And, when Twm's own body is found,

> a fortnight gone
> Was the shy soul from the festering flesh and bone
> When they found him there, entombed in the lucid weather.
>
> (pp. 37–41)[6]

Here, even amid the grim facts, there is room at least for ambivalence. There is a hint of sense in it all, for, although 'airy tomb' describes a life which, in obvious ways, enslaves Twm, it also suggests a necessary dwelling-place for his soul which afforded some room to breathe. He rests, at the end, in lucid weather. Nevertheless, all we have is a hint of an enduring sense, little more. Whether it is more than a sense of endurance remains to be seen.

The most direct challenge to the priest who has to mediate the teachings of the Church to such people is expressed in 'A Priest to his People'. Moelwyn Merchant recalls that R. S. Thomas once told him 'that his most vivid response to the peninsula of Llŷn was not to the Christian remains but to the archaeology, the geology behind them'.[7] The Christian revelation comes face to face with an older paganism. At first the priest is irritably impatient:

> Men of the hills, wantoners, men of Wales,
> With your sheep and your pigs and your ponies, your sweaty
> females
> How I have hated you for your irreverence, your scorn even
> Of the refinements of art and the mysteries of the Church . . . .
>
> ('A Priest to his People')

But when he tries to chastise them he finds his words fail when confronted by something they have to offer:

I whose invective would spurt like a flame of fire
To be quenched always in the coldness of your stare.

In fact, when he reflects on the lives they lead, the priest is not at
all confident that what he has to offer is better than what they
already possess. He is not blind to what they lack, but he is
forced to ask their forgiveness for his initial impatience. He is
obsessed by these people, an obsession no less intense because of
the ambivalence which characterises it.

You are curt and graceless, yet your sudden laughter
Is sharp and bright as a whipped pool,
When the wind strikes or the clouds are flying;
And all the devices of church and school
Have failed to cripple your unhallowed movements,
Or put a halter on your wild soul.
You are lean and spare, yet your strength is a mockery
Of the pale words in the black Book,
And why should you come like sparrows for prayer crumbs,
Whose hands can dabble in the world's blood?

I have taxed your ignorance of rhyme and sonnet,
Your want of deference to the painter's skill,
But I know, as I listen, that your speech has in it
The source of all poetry, clear as a rill
Bubbling from your lips; and what brushwork could equal
The artistry of your dwelling on the bare hill?
You will forgive, then, my initial hatred,
My first intolerance of your uncouth ways,
You who are indifferent to all that I can offer,
Caring not whether I blame or praise.
With your pigs and your sheep and your sons
    and holly-cheeked daughters
You will still continue to unwind your days
In a crude tapestry under the jealous heavens
To affront, bewilder, yet compel my gaze.

(pp. 29–30)

I have already referred to the fact that the farmer's endurance
is enacted under 'curious stars'. What sense is to be found in his
relentless struggle? In the poem we have just considered, not

only are the stars curious, the heavens are jealous. This endured toil and suffering itself extracts a respect from a religion which wants to make something more of it. Yet, we have little indication in this first volume of what that 'something more' can be. The very attempt to give it a content comes under severe threat from the life which surrounds the priest. The description of the church at Manafon reflects the fragility which seems to characterise the Faith.

> The church stands, built from the river stone,
> Brittle with light, as though a breath could shatter
> Its slender frame.
> > ('Country Church')

The nature of the land and the life it sustains challenges and resists the mediation of the Christian mysteries.

> But though soft flowers break
> In delicate waves round limbs the river fashioned
> With so smooth care, no friendly God has cautioned
> The brimming tides of fescue for its sake.

By the end of the first volume, then, we have seen the challenge which faces the Christian religion. There is, as yet, little indication of how that challenge is to be met. The peasant greets the poet but the meaning of his gesture is as ambivalent and uncertain as the religious response, which, as yet, is struggling to emerge.

> No speech; the raised hand affirms
> All that is left unsaid
> By the mute tongue and the unmoistened lips:
> The land's patience and a tree's
> Knotted endurance and
> The heart's doubt whether to curse or bless,
> All packed into a single gesture.
> > ('Peasant Greeting', p. 28)

Whether to curse or to bless? That question not only haunts the peasant. It haunts the priest and the poet too. The title of R. S. Thomas's first volume is taken from the Book of Job: 'For thou shalt be in league with the stones of the field'. Yet, given the tensions and ambivalences we have witnessed in the poems, no sure relationships emerge. The gestures which come from peasant, priest and poet also seem to pack into themselves meanings which cannot be reconciled. Yet, T. S. Eliot has shown us what is at stake: 'We may say that religion, as distinguished from modern paganism, implies a life in conformity with nature . . . a wrong attitude towards nature implies, somewhere, a wrong attitude towards God, and that the consequence is an inevitable doom.'[8] But what is the right attitude to nature? That question is posed, but not answered, by the poet at this stage.

2   Earth to Earth

Moelwyn Merchant has argued that *An Acre of Land* (1952) marks a new relation between the poet and Iago Prytherch exemplified in the poem 'Memories'. It may well be true that the poem marks an attempt at a new beginning, but it must be remembered that, although the poem is placed first in those selected for the collection *Song at the Year's Turning*, it is the final poem of the original volume. So far from the hope of a new beginning pervading *An Acre of Land*, it is little more than mentioned at the end of it. The hope is one expressed in face of the formidable difficulties posed by the peasant's situation. It is the difficulties we remember, at the end of the volume, rather than the hope. For the poet–priest, as we have seen, the difficulties stand in the way of a mediation of religious sense.

We are tempted to see the peasant's way of life in romantic terms.

> The sheep are grazing at Bwlch-y-Fedwen,
> Arranged romantically in the usual manner
> On a bleak background of bald stone.
> ('The Welsh Hill Country')

But the grim realities are beyond the romantic reader's comprehension.

> Too far, too far to see
> The set of his eyes and the slow phthisis
> Wasting his frame under the ripped coat,
> There's a man still farming at Ty'n-y-Fawnog,
> Contributing grimly to the accepted pattern,
> The embryo music dead in his throat.[1]

The accepted pattern is such that the poet has no difficulty in understanding the depopulation of the hills. On the contrary, his

11

own advice is uncompromising: 'Leave it, leave it' ('Depopulation of the Hills', p. 52). But he is advocating leaving more than the farm. The poet has, in a sense, grown impatient with his subject. He despairs of extracting any sense from the peasant's situation. Yet, born of this very despair is a compassion for the peasant; a compassion also born of the realisation that he can do nothing for the peasant and that his interest in him constitutes an intrusion. Even the poet's amusement in seeing the farmer's new machine,

> Ah, you should see Cynddylan on a tractor.
> Gone the old look that yoked him to the soil;
> He's a new man now, part of the machine
>   ('Cynddylan on a Tractor')

is tempered by the realisation of the price the peasant pays for progress:

> The sun comes over the tall trees
> Kindling all the hedges, but not for him
> Who runs his engine on a different fuel.
> And all the birds are singing, bills wide in vain,
> As Cynddylan passes proudly up the lane.
>   (p. 54)

There is a hint of the possibility of a celebration of the rising sun and the singing birds, but what predominates in *An Acre of Land* is the harshness of the peasant's life. The poet is amazed at Iago Prytherch's persistence.[2] The Hill Farmer makes a direct appeal to the poet and to us:

> I am the farmer, stripped of love
> And thought and grace by the land's hardness;
> But what I am saying over the fields'
> Desolate acres, rough with dew,
> Is, Listen, listen, I am a man like you.
>   ('The Hill Farmer Speaks', p. 55)

But the listening can itself contribute no redeeming sense to this scene, one whose end is all to familiar:

> You remember Davies? He died, you know,
> With his face to the wall, as the manner is
> Of the poor peasant in his stone croft
> On the Welsh hills.
>
> ('Death of a Peasant')

The neighbours of the unfortunate man, like the poet, are devoid of words of comfort:

> The bare floor without a rug
> Or mat to soften the loud tread
> Of neighbours crossing the uneasy boards
> To peer at Davies with gruff words
> Of meaningless comfort, before they turned
> Heartless away from the stale smell
> Of death in league with those dank walls.
>
> (p. 59)

How, then, can any religious sense be mediated in this bleak landscape? It is true that R. S. Thomas salutes those who endure with resignation, but often they do not even achieve the hopes Freud entertained for his 'honest smallholders' who were to face life without the consolations of religion. Here is Freud's hope:

> And, as for the great necessities of Fate, against which there is no help, they will learn to endure with resignation. Of what use to them is the mirage of wide acres in the moon, whose harvest no one has ever yet seen? As honest smallholders on this earth they will know how to cultivate their plot in such a way that it supports them.[3]

If worldy prosperity is the norm, R. S. Thomas's peasants, for the most part, do not cultivate their plot in such a way that it supports them. There is a kind of grim sense in working the soil, but the movement is a downward one, devoid of transcendental implications.

> A field with tall hedges and a young
> Moon in the branches and one star
> Declining westward set the scene

> Where he works slowly astride the rows
> Of red mangolds and green swedes
> Plying mechanically his cold blade.
>
> This is his world, the hedge defines
> The mind's limits; only the sky
> Is boundless, and he never looks up;
> His gaze is deep in the dark soil,
> As are his feet. The soil is all;
> His hands fondle it, and his bones
> Are formed out of it with the swedes.
> And if sometimes the knife errs,
> Burying itself in his shocked flesh,
> Then out of the wound the blood seeps home
> To the warm soil from which it came.
>
> ('Soil'[4])

If the hedge defines the limits of the peasant's mind, how is anything else to break in on it? The peasant never looks up at the boundless sky. What hope is there for him? Is there a clear answer?

> Blind? Yes, and deaf, and dumb, and the last irks most,
> For could he speak, would not the glib tongue boast
> A lore denied our neoteric sense,
> Being handed down from the age of innocence?
> Or would the cracked lips, parted at last, disclose
> The embryonic thought that never grows?
>
> ('Enigma', p. 68)

There are moments when the thought seems to be more explicit, expressed in the farmer's relation to the changing seasons. As summer comes,

> His blood grows hot, the singing cloak of flies,
> Worn each day, bears witness; the stones ring
> Fierce echoes of his heat; he meets himself
> Everywhere in the smell of the ripe earth.
>
> ('Summer', p. 67)

But the poet has doubts. Does the peasant possess a wisdom

denied to more refined sensibilities, or is the poet imposing a knowledge on the peasant which he does not possess?

No matter how this question is to be answered, the poet realises that he has to revise some of his assumptions concerning the peasant's way of life. It is insufficient simply to note the peasant's surroundings and take for granted that they will have a certain significance for him. It is in this taking for granted that the poet's hopes are frustrated.

> You failed me, farmer, I was afraid you would
> The day I saw you loitering with the cows,
> Yourself one of them but for the smile,
> Vague as moonlight, cast upon your face
> From some dim source, whose nature I mistook.
> The hills had grace, the light clothed them
> With wild beauty, so that I thought,
> Watching the pattern of your slow wake
> Through seas of dew, that you yourself
> Wore that same beauty by the right of birth.
> ('Valediction')

Yet, although he accuses the peasant of failing him, he also recognises his own confusions. The meaning of the peasant's relation to his surroundings is itself a matter of mediation. Nature will not have an unambiguous immediate causal effect on those who confront it, such that a meaningful relation to it is generated and made secure. On the contrary, people may stand in a number of different relations to nature. To appreciate this fact we need to see how nature enters people's lives. The poet has assumed that nature must enter those lives in certain determinate ways, and is annoyed when the fact of the peasant's life contradicts this assumption.

He is also annoyed, however, because he has suffered at the peasant's hands:

> I know now, many a time since
> Hurt by your spite or guile that is more sharp
> Than stinging hail and treacherous
> As white frost forming after a day
> Of smiling warmth, that your uncouthness has
> No kinship with the earth, where all is forgiven,

> All is requited in the seasonal round
> Of sun and rain, healing the year's scars.

The lack of kinship between the peasant and nature means that a certain kind of salvation is denied him.

> The two things
> That could redeem your ignorance, the beauty
> And grace that trees and flowers labour to teach,
> Were never yours, you shut your heart against them.
> You stopped your ears to the soft influence
> Of birds, preferring the dull tone
> Of the thick blood, the loud, unlovely rattle
> Of mucous in the throat, the shallow stream
> Of neighbours' trivial talk.

In this poem, the poet concentrates on the triviality of the peasant's concerns. Of course, scenes of natural beauty can often have the effect of placing some squabble or other in the proper light of pettiness. The sense which nature has in that context is mediated via that revelation. But the difficulty which the poet–priest has to face is that the facts of the peasant's life to which he has drawn our attention are *not* trivialities. The relentless harshness of the peasant's burdens cannot be placed in the same category as petty squabbles. What does a kinship with the earth have to do with these harsh realities? How is all forgiven in face of them? As yet, R. S. Thomas has given us no answer in verse to these questions. Roland Mathias thinks that the poet is confused in thinking that there is a necessary connection between the grace of natural beauty and inward grace.

> The grace of flowers, of hills, of the village boy . . . is a physical quality, of outline, of appearance, of movement, aesthetically satisfying the observer's eye. It has no necessary relationship to an inward grace (grace in the theological context) a spiritual quality necessary to turn the heart away from spite and guile.[5]

We have already seen why the connection cannot be *necessary*; why it is confused to assume that, if one is placed in the presence of natural grace, inward grace will follow automatically. We have already seen that R. S. Thomas recognises that confusion himself. Roland Mathias is puzzled by this, since he too recognises that R. S. Thomas must be familiar with the distinction he is making. The trouble comes from the fact that Roland Mathias's observation misses the deeper issues involved here. R. S. Thomas is concerned *not* simply with natural grace, 'the beauty and grace that trees and flowers labour to teach', present though it is, but with grace in nature; a grace 'where all is forgiven'. How is *that* grace to be mediated through the detail of the peasant's experience? That is the question that lurks in these poems and which is to become more prominent in later volumes. That is why, faced with a burst of indignation from the poet in face of the peasant's triviality, we feel that, more explicit though the reaction is than anything encountered so far, it will not last.

> For this I leave you
> Alone in your harsh acres, herding pennies
> Into a sock to serve you for a pillow
> Through the long night that waits upon your span.
> (pp. 65–6)

By the end of *An Acre of Land*, we see the poet wanting to re-establish relations with Iago Prytherch, to attempt once again to sing of the relation between the peasant and the land. The peasant's lips may be sealed, but is there not a rich harvest of which the poet can sing on his behalf?

> Come, Iago, my friend, and let us stand together
> Now in the time of the mild weather,
> Before the wind changes and the winter brings
> The leprous frost to the fields, and I will sing
> The land's praises, making articulate
> Your strong feelings, your thoughts of no date,
> Your secret learning, innocent of books.
> ('Memories', p. 45)

This is not the last time the poet will stand with Prytherch. If we felt his irritation with the peasant would not last, this offer of unqualified friendship is itself too good to last. Both reactions are unambiguous and cannot therefore reflect the complex relationship between the poet–priest and the peasant. He will return to this subject again and again, but he does not know why. His inability to know this is an aspect of his lack of clarity regarding how his situation is to be understood. He is convinced that there is something, important to him as poet and priest, which is to be wrested from the peasant's condition, but at the end of *An Acre of Land* he has no clear idea of what that 'something' is.

When I was young, I went to school
With pencil and foot-rule
Sponge and slate,
And sat on a tall stool
At learning's gate.

When I was older, the gate swung wide;
Clever and keen-eyed
In I pressed,
But found in the mind's pride
No peace, no rest.

Then who was it taught me back to go
To cattle and barrow,
Field and plough;
To keep to the one furrow,
As I do now?

('The One Furrow'[6])

Three years later R. S. Thomas brought selections from *The Stones of the Field* and *An Acre of Land* together in the collection *Song at the Year's Turning* (1955). The later poems added to the collection bear witness to the direction in which I have suggested the poet's development was moving.

The priest is still confronted by the peasant who is a slave to the earth, but he now lets the peasant speak to him with a new directness which compels sympathy: 'No offence, friend; it was the earth that did it.' The peasant thinks he is beyond hope:

She dragged me down,
Slurring my gait first, then my speech.
I never loved her, there's no ring
Binding us; but it's too late now.
I am branded upon the brow
With muck, as though I were her slave.

('The Slave', p. 104)

The poet sees that if this verdict is not to be endorsed, there has to be some way in which bonds can be forged between a grace in nature and the brand on the peasant's brow. Grace cannot be grace unless it is capable of informing this condition.

> Is there blessing? Light's peculiar grace
> In cold splendour robes this tortured place
> For strange marriage. Voices in the wind
> Weave a garland where a mortal sinned.
> Winter rots you; who is there to blame?
> The new grass shall purge you in its flame.
> ('Song at the Year's Turning'[7])

At this stage, the marriage which has to be mediated between grace and the peasant's condition seems indeed to be a strange one. But at least the poet–priest realises how essential such mediation is. Nature is not going to do the task for him. It seems there has to be an act of purgation. He recognises, even more explicitly, what was wrong with his earlier assumptions.

> You must revise
> Your bland philosophy of nature, earth
> Has of itself no power to make men wise.
> ('Autumn on the Land', p. 106)

The mediation of sense must take account of a whole range of facts. Those which constitute obstacles to religion range from trivialities to various forms of affliction. Prytherch has become rich and his new attitudes distance him even further from any kind of grace.[8] Even within nature there are harsh facts which any talk of grace would have to take into account, yet 'without that indulgence of violence the poetry of Ted Hughes sometimes suggests'.[9]

> The fox drags its wounded belly
> Over the snow, the crimson seeds
> Of blood burst with a mild explosion,
> Soft as excrement, bold as roses.
>
> Over the snow that feels no pity,
> Whose white hands can give no healing,
> The fox drags its wounded belly.
> ('January', p. 107)

How can there be grace in nature if there is no pity or healing? It seems as if the poet is faced with building a bridge between two irreconcilables, grace on the one hand and various forms of affliction on the other. Yet, if that is how the problem is conceived, perhaps there is no answer to it. Perhaps it is confused to think that we must first postulate the irreconcilable elements and then subsequently try to build the bridge between them. Perhaps the idea of God must itself incorporate, from the outset, those elements which we confusedly suppose are incompatible with it. R. S. Thomas begins to explore this new possibility in a poem where, it is suggested, God is related not only to the lighter, but *also* to the darker side of life.

> Who said to the trout,
> You shall die on Good Friday
> To be food for a man
> And his pretty lady?
>
> It was I, said God,
> Who formed the roses
> In the delicate flesh
> And the tooth that bruises.
> ('Pisces'[10])

R. S. Thomas has said of himself, 'I play on a small pipe, a little aside from the main road. But thank you for listening.' But, in the small geographical area he has mapped out for himself, a decisive drama is to be played out. It is the drama of concept formation in religion; the attempt to see whether or how religious belief can inform human life. The solitary place, which may be thought of as unimportant in terms of business and commerce, can nevertheless be saluted as the place in which this essential drama is to be enacted.

> Scarcely a street, too few houses
> To merit the title; just a way between
> The one tavern and the one shop
> That leads nowhere and fails at the top
> Of the short hill, eaten away
> By long erosion of the green tide
> Of grass creeping perpetually nearer
> This last outpost of time past.

So little happens; the black dog
Cracking his fleas in the hot sun
Is history. Yet the girl who crosses
From door to door moves to a scale
Beyond the bland day's two dimensions.

Stay, then, village, for round you spins
On slow axis a world as vast
And meaningful as any poised
By great Plato's solitary mind.

('The Village'[11])

And so, in his village, the poet–priest watches and prays. He has
to pray for those peasants who waste away not only in body, but
in soul, mind and spirit too. Questions come to him, but God
silences them, the God,

Who sees you suffer and me pray
And touches you with the sun's ray,
That heals not, yet blinds my eyes
And seals my lips as Job's were sealed
Imperiously in the old days.

('Priest and Peasant', p. 109)

These statements are full of ambiguity. Job's lips were sealed
because he came to see that his questions, his request for
justifications from God, though natural, were, in the end, mis-
conceived. 'It is the will of God', for Job, was not an answer to
his questions, but a working through them in such a way that he
did not want to ask them any more.[12] It is not clear, here,
whether the poet has achieved that 'working through'. We feel
that his questions are still there, a fact to which the further
volumes of his verse testify. The use of the word 'Imperiously'
also suggests questions put down rather than worked through.
On the other hand, questions can be silenced by a sense of the
majesty of God. Such tensions in the poems are not to be
resolved or tidied up. They reflect the poet's relation in verse to
the questions which bear in on him. He is acutely aware of the
dangers involved in the composition of poetry on such themes.
There are grave risks involved. There is no guarantee of success.
Worse, there is the constant possibility of causing harm and

damage. In approaching Iago Prytherch yet again, the poet, in making him speak for himself, is able to voice through him all the concern he feels about the dangers of poetry. So far from casting light on the way of life Prytherch leads, the poetry may amount to no more than a distorting intrusion into the very subject it wishes to illuminate. Worse, the failure may be such that the way of life thus publicised may never be the same again. These fears are expressed in Prytherch's reaction to the poet:

> I am Prytherch. Forgive me. I don't know
> What you are talking about; your thoughts flow
> Too swiftly for me; I cannot dawdle
> Along their banks and fish in their quick stream
> With crude fingers. I am alone, exposed
> In my own fields with no place to run
> From your sharp eyes. I, who a moment back
> Paddled in the bright grass, the old farm
> Warm as a sack about me, feel the cold
> Winds of the world blowing. The patched gate
> You left open will never be shut again.
>
> ('Invasion on the Farm'[13])

Yet, suddenly, unexpectedly, among these poems comes one which stands out from them all, even more than 'Pisces'. At first, we are presented with the by now familiar, perhaps over-familiar, predicament of the priest who can find no answers to the questions for religion posed by the life he sees around him.

> To one kneeling down no word came,
> Only the wind's song saddening the lips
> Of the grave saints, rigid in glass;
> Or the dry whisper of unseen wings,
> Bats not angels, in the high roof.
>
> ('In a Country Church')

But, then, suddenly, this:

> Was he balked by silence? He kneeled long,
> And saw love in a dark crown
> Of thorns blazing, and a winter tree
> Golden with fruit of a man's body.[14]

The vision is a marvellous one, but in relation to the poems we have encountered so far in R. S. Thomas's work, it stands out in stark contrast. But this is to be the poet's task of mediation in verse: the unenviable one of showing how love can blaze in a dark crown of thorns, or how a winter tree can be made golden by the fruit of a man's body.

At this stage, however, the poet feels that, on the whole, he has failed in his task. He feels he has not yet found a way to work through to a sustained religious sense in things, although the earth and its challenge continue to compel his gaze.

> All in vain, I will cease now
> My long absorption with the plough,
> With the tame and the wild creatures
> And man united with the earth.
> I have failed after many seasons
> To bring truth to birth,
> And nature's simple equations
> In the mind's precincts do not apply.
>
> But where to turn? Earth endures
> After the passing, necessary shame
> Of winter, and the old lie
> Of green places beckons me still
> From the new world, ugly and evil,
> That men pry for in truth's name.
>   ('No Through Road'[15])

3 Testing the Spirits

In 1952, R. S. Thomas wrote a satirical dramatic poem for radio called *The Minister*. It completes the poems included in *Song at the Year's Turning*. Speaking of it, Moelwyn Merchant says, 'This story has none of the subtle striving of the country priest, attempting to graft a rich tradition of liturgy and creed upon a tough upland stock; this is the struggle of a bitter casuistry picking its way between tact and truth.'[1] I do not want to deny the latter description, but is not the former with which he contrasts it a misleading picture of the poems we have encountered hitherto? There is reason to believe that R. S. Thomas finds a more generous conception of grace in the Catholic tradition than that he finds offered in the Protestantism of Luther and Calvin. On the other hand, we cannot argue that R. S. Thomas wants to contrast a narrow Nonconformity beset with problems, with different traditions, rich in creed and liturgy. Whether a liturgy is rich cannot be determined by considerations internal to the liturgy. A liturgy becomes a dead letter unless it speaks to the people to whom it is said. There is no reason to think that R. S. Thomas is not faced with problems in the mediation of the liturgy which are as severe as the problems which face Nonconformity. After all, the majority of the poems on these themes concern the meeting of a *priest* and his people. What is true is that Nonconformity may have special problems of its own. The problems in Nonconformity R. S. Thomas emphasises are none too subtle, which is not to say they are not real. That is partly why the satire in *The Minister* often takes a comic turn in highlighting the trivialisation of religion.

From the outset of his dramatic poem, R. S. Thomas locates the issue facing Nonconformity as one of mediation of sense.

> In the hill country at the moor's edge
> There is a chapel, religion's outpost
> In the untamed land west of the valleys,

24

The marginal land where flesh meets spirit
Only on Sundays and the days between
Are mortgaged to the grasping soil.
(*The Minister*, p. 12²)

The harshness of life in the hills and the attitudes of the people
fashioned by it determine the parameters within which God's
word, if it is to be God's word, has to speak. But what hope is
there of effective speech?

"Beloved, let us love one another," the words are blown
To pieces by the unchristened wind
In the chapel rafters, and love's text
Is riddled by the inhuman cry
Of buzzards circling above the moor.

(p. 13)

The obstacles are also found in attitudes to be found from within
religion itself; for example, in the attitudes of deacons to minis-
ters as depicted by R. S. Thomas.

They chose their pastors as they chose their horses
For hard work. But the last one died
Sooner than they expected; nothing sinister,
You understand, but just the natural
Breaking of the heart beneath a load
Unfit for horses. 'Ay, he's a good 'un',
Job Davies had said; and Job was a master
Hand at choosing a nag or a pastor.

(Ibid.)

As R. S. Thomas said, 'They all forgot that even a pastor is a
man first and a minister after.' Surrounding the chapel is a
natural world which, in times past, has been seen as a celebra-
tion of God. So well-established were such possibilities of cele-
bration that, as the poet tells us with gentle humour, a certain
comic possessiveness concerning God developed out of it: 'Wales
in fact is His peculiar home'. But, then, the poet asks the vital
question as far as the mediation of a religious sense is concerned:

> But where is that voice now?
> Is it in the chapel vestry, where Davies is using
> The logic of the Smithfield?
>
> (p. 14)

That logic is exemplified in the sinister pragmatism of Job
Davies, the deacon, as he discusses the kind of minister he wants
for the chapel:

> A young 'un we want, someone young
> Without a wife. Let him learn
> His calling first, and choose after
> Among our girls, if he must marry.
> There's your girl, Pugh; or yours, Parry;
> Ministers' wives they ought to be
> With those white hands that are too soft
> For lugging muck or pulling a cow's
> Tits. But ay, he must be young.
> Remember that mare of yours, John?
>
> Too old when you bought her; the old sinner
> Had had a taste of the valleys first
> And never took to the rough grass
> In the top fields. You could do nothing
> With her, but let her go her way.
> Lucky you sold her. But you can't sell
> Ministers, so we must have a care
> In choosing. Take my advice,
> Pick someone young, and I'll soon show him
> How things is managed in the hills here.
>
> (p. 15)

Davies is richer than the other farmers and takes his success to
be itself a sign of divine favour. Grace and worldly prosperity
walk hand in hand. An older paganism, on the other hand, used
nature very differently:

> There were people here before these,
> Measuring truth according to the moor's
> Pitiless commentary and the wind's veto.
> Out in the moor there is a bone whitening,
> Worn smooth by the long dialectic

Of rain and sunlight. What has that to do
With choosing a minister? Nothing, nothing.
(p. 16)

And yet, if the good news of the Christian Gospel is to speak to
the people who live in these hills, these natural facts will have to
tell of God somehow or other. We cannot think of men placed in
these circumstances as we think of the animals. There are
obviously important and essential differences between them; not
least, 'the teasings of eternity'.

> The cow goes round and round the field,
> Bored with its grass world, and in its eyes
> The mute animal hunger, which you pity,
> You the confirmed sentimentalist,
> Playing the old anthropomorphic game.
> But for the cow, it is the same world over the hedge.
> No one ever teased her with pictures of flyless meadows,
> Where the grass is eternally green
> No matter how often the tongue bruises it,
> Or the dung soils it.
>
> But with man it is otherwise.
(p. 17)

So the hedge does not define the mind's limits after all.[3] There is
talk of a world other than this one, a somewhere else in terms of
which this world is given such sense as it has. But, again, the
question is of how such talk is to inform the lives people lead. In
R. S. Thomas's poem we are given a picture of the minister who
has been chosen as pastor of the chapel in the hills. He is the
person, in the Nonconformist tradition, who has been called to
preach the message. When we look at the minister's conception
of his vocation, however, further difficulties await us.

When R. S. Thomas lets the young minister, the Reverend
Elias Morgan, BA, speak for himself, we can see, almost from the
outset, why his ministry is doomed to failure. He does notice
some facts of nature, such as the return of curlews at nesting-
time and is disturbed by the fact that people seem too busy to
pay attention to such facts. On the other hand, his own knowl-
edge and interest in nature is extremely limited. How, then, is
he to minister to country people?

> I wore a black coat, being fresh from college,
> With striped trousers, and, indeed, my knowledge
> Would have been complete, had it included
> The bare moor, where nature brooded
> Over her old, inscrutable secret.
> But I didn't even know the names
> Of the birds and the flowers by which one gets
> A little closer to nature's heart.
>
> (p. 19)

Nevertheless, the singing of a thrush disturbs him, since it seems to tell him of something which cannot be captured within the confines of his narrow theology.

> Its singing troubled my young mind
> With strange theories, pagan but sweet,
> That made the Book's black letters dance
> To a tune John Calvin never heard.
> The evening sunlight on the wall
> Of my room was a new temptation.
> Luther would have thrown his Bible at it.
> I closed my eyes, and went on with my sermon.
>
> (Ibid.)

The content, indeed, the very possibility of his sermon depends on closing his eyes and his heart to what nature is striving to tell him. He turns away from nature.

> A few flowers bloomed beneath the window,
> Set there once by a kind hand
> In the old days, a woman's gesture
> Of love against the childless years.
> Morgan pulled them up; they were untidy.
> He sprinkled cinders there instead.
>
> (Ibid.)

Given all this, how could his ministry appear to be so successful at first? To see how this was possible, it is necessary to appreciate that Elias Morgan and his congregation are in the grip of a kind of religious romanticism. They are guilty of what Kierkegaard calls a foreshortening of eternity. It consists essentially of the desire to take eternity by storm, the thought that spirituality or salvation can be grasped once and for all in a moment. A romantic example of such foreshortening would be the assumption that love could be made secure in the exchange of a glance or in a single touch. An artistic example of such foreshortening would be the assumption that a work of art can be replaced by a 'happening'. Kierkegaard, in *Purity of Heart*,[4] makes the point by referring to a man who admired the beauty and proportions of a map. There was only one thing wrong with this man; he did not realise that a map is meant to be used. So when he was put down in the heart of the country, with its many miles of winding, unkept roads, dismay overtook him. He wanted to foreshorten eternity, to possess it once and for all in a rapturous gaze on the map. He was not prepared to travel.[5] Such is the theology and sermonising of R. S. Thomas's minister. His sermon rages against sin and the congregation thrill under its lash, but the sentiments they experience are unmediated in the rest of their lives and are therefore devoid of any serious religious significance.

> Who is this opening and closing the Book
> With a bang, and pointing a finger
> Before him in accusation?
> Who is this leaning from the wide pulpit
> In judgment, and filling the chapel
> With sound as God fills the sky?
> Is that his shadow on the wall behind?
> Shout on Morgan. You'll be nothing to-morrow.
>
> (p. 20)

He can be nothing tomorrow because his experiences will not give tomorrow sense for him. They are ephemeral and transient. But that is precisely the kind of experiences the minister's congregation want too; the kind of experiences which can give elation within the confines of the chapel, but which are unmediated in the detail of everyday life and hence make no serious demands on them. Even among those who are carried away with emotion in this way, there are some who know how to temper it with pragmatic realism.

The people were pleased with their new pastor;
Their noses dripped and the blood ran faster
Along their veins, as the hot sparks
Fell from his lips on their dry thoughts:
The whole chapel was soon ablaze.
Except for the elders, and even they were moved
By the holy tumult, but not extremely.
They knew better than that.

(Ibid.)

Despite the pride, envy, malice and backbiting, sin, as usual, was defined in terms of sex and money. This is what the preacher railed against although it has little effect on what actually happens. The deacon Davies is eyeing the young Buddug. The minister thinks of effective preaching in terms of the fervour, the *hwyl*, which he can whip himself into in his sermon.

I was good that night, I had the *hwyl*.
We sang the verses of the last hymn
Twice. We might have had a revival
If only the organ had kept in time.
But that was the organist's fault.
I went to my house with the light heart
Of one who had made a neat job
Of pruning the branches on the tree
Of good and evil. Llywarch came with me
As far as the gate. Who was the girl
Who smiled at me as she slipped by?

(p. 22)

There is marvellous humour in the suggestion that men's coming to God depends on the organ keeping in tune. It is the Nonconformist parallel to the foreshortening of eternity Miguel de Unamuno found in the aestheticism of the Catholic religious processions he witnessed as a child, an aestheticism which led him to say, 'My soul was nourished on perfume.' The Welsh Nonconformist might say, 'My soul was nourished on *hwyl* and hymns.' When Morgan does try to apply even his restricted conception of morality by confronting Davies with his affair with Buddug, the Davies who supplies the food which is part of the minister's pay, he soon finds what is expected of him.

Davies

Adultery's a big word, Morgans; where's your proof?
You who never venture from under your roof
Once the night's come; the blinds all down
For fear of the moon's bum rubbing the window.
Take a word from me and keep your nose
In the Black Book, so it won't be tempted
To go sniffing where it's not wanted.

(p. 26)

Like Kierkegaard's map-reader, R. S. Thomas's minister is set down in the heart of the country and he finds that his *hwyl* does not travel well. It does not speak to what he sees around him. It does not speak because he does not see how the relentless seasons tell of God. Instead he tries to apply the lessons of his university degree to the hill people. He holds a religious discussion group (a *seiat*), and a Bible class, but no one comes. Now and again there are moments of tenderness, of course, and they give him hope that tomorrow will be different:

But the morrow woke me
To the ancestral fury of the rain
Spitting and clawing at the pane.
I looked out on a grey world, grey with despair.

(p. 30)

Slowly, surely, Morgan becomes part of the place and keeps his silence. But the price is high, for his words cannot speak, his language is impotent:

I knew it all,
Although I never pried, I knew it all.
I knew why Buddug was away from chapel.
I knew that Pritchard, the *Fron*, watered his milk.
I knew who put the ferret with the fowls
In Pugh's hen-house. I knew and pretended I didn't.
And they knew that I knew and pretended I didn't.
They listened to me preaching the unique gospel
Of love; but our eyes never met. And outside
The blood of God darkened the evening sky.

(pp. 30–1)

The minister is elated at big funerals. He sees Llywarch lying in his coffin and half hopes it had been Job Davies!

There is no doubt that R. S. Thomas thinks that Protestantism has much to answer for in Wales. He sees it as a vehicle for a foreshortening of eternity. He might well see there what amounts to the Manichean heresy – the belief that all physical things are evil and that the infinite should be approached directly without the mediation of matter. Morgan the minister ignored the natural world which surrounded him. He thought that *hwyl* was the medium by which the infinite can be approached directly.

The Catholic novelist, short-story writer and essayist Flannery O'Connor in commenting on the Manichean heresy says,

> The Manicheans separated spirit and matter. To them all material things were evil. They sought pure spirit and tried to approach the infinite directly without any mediation of matter. This is pretty much the modern spirit . . . .[6]

She had little doubt what effect this has on our understanding of religious belief:

> The problem of the novelist who wishes to write about a man's encounter with this God is how he shall make the experience – which is both natural and supernatural – understandable, and credible, to his reader. In any age this would be a problem, but in our own, it is a well-nigh unsurmountable one. Today's audience is one in which religious feeling has become, if not atrophied, at least vaporous and sentimental. When Emerson decided, in 1832, that he could no longer celebrate the Lord's Supper unless the bread and wine were removed, an important step in the vaporization of religion in America was taken, and the spirit of that step has continued apace. When the physical fact is separated from the spiritual reality, the dissolution of belief is eventually inevitable.[7]

Similar sentiments are expressed by R. S. Thomas:

> It was upon the simple things of life that Jesus based his message, the sower and the seed, the shepherd and his flock. When he wished to institute a service which could express and convey the essence of his teaching, he took bread and wine and

consecrated them metaphors of that love and sacrifice which
are of the very essence of eternal life.[8]

When a religion ignores the mediation of the spiritual in the
physical, R. S. Thomas's verdict is unequivocal:

> Is there no passion in Wales? There is none
> Except in the racked hearts of men like Morgan,
> Condemned to wither and starve in the cramped cell
> Of thought their fathers made them.
> Protestantism – the adroit castrator
> Of art; the bitter negation
> Of song and dance and the heart's innocent joy –
> You have botched our flesh and left us only the soul's
> Terrible impotence in a warm world.
>
> Need we go on? In spite of all
> His courage Morgan could not avert
> His failure, for he chose to fight
> With that which yields to nothing human.
> He never listened to the hills'
> Music calling to the hushed
> Music within; but let his mind
> Fester with brooding on the sly
> Infirmities of the hill people.
> The pus conspired with the old
> Infection lurking in his breast.

> (p. 31)

The poem ends with the narrator commending the direction in
which Morgan and his congregation could have turned, but did
not.

> In the chapel acre there is a grave,
> And grass contending with the stone
> For mastery of the near horizon,
> And on the stone words; but never mind them:
> Their formal praise is a vain gesture
> Against the moor's encroaching tide.
> We will listen instead to the wind's text
> Blown through the roof, or the thrush's song
> In the thick bush that proved him wrong,

Wrong from the start, for nature's truth
Is primary and her changing seasons
Correct out of a vaster reason
The vague errors of the flesh.

(p. 32)

'Wrong from the start': that is a harsh verdict, but a necessary
one. For that is the heart of the problem of mediating a religious
sense – the issue of how to start! The issue of concept formation
in religion is precisely the question of what sort of hold religious
belief has on human life. It is in relation to the kind of hold
religion has, as shown in *The Minister*, that R. S. Thomas is
saying, 'Wrong from the start'. But what of the alternative, the
nature which provides hints of a 'vaster reason' to correct 'The
vague errors of the flesh'? Does R. S. Thomas's dramatic poem
actually show us what sense the alternative could have? I think
not. We have a promise of a mediation of sense, but no actual
example of it. The struggle for the emergence of such mediation
in verse will characterise the poet's further volumes.

4 An Inadequate Language?

In *Poetry for Supper* (1958), *Tares* (1961) and *The Bread of Truth* (1964) R. S. Thomas pays more direct attention to the difficulties he encounters in trying to speak of God with meaning. It is not that he does not revert to moods and sentiments we have met with already; he certainly does. But he also expresses a growing concern with his own vocation as a priest, a concern out of which maturer religious understandings are to emerge in later volumes.

In *Poetry for Supper*, the poet confesses that the figure of Prytherch still calls out to him with all the many challenges such a call involves. But how are those challenges to be taken up? Does the poet possess an adequate language in which to do so?

> could the talk begin
> Where it left off? Have I not been
> Too long away?
>
> ('Temptation of a Poet')

The poet fears that he lacks the resources to continue their conversation:

> Prytherch, I am undone;
> The past calls with the cool smell
> Of autumn leaves, but the mind draws
> Me onward blind with the world's dust,
> Seeking a spring that my heart fumbles.
>
> (p. 14)[1]

He knows well enough, by now, the styles in which genuine religious faith cannot be found. His disdain for such people as Job Davies, the deacon, remains.

> Who put that crease in your soul,
> Davies, ready this fine morning

> For the staid chapel, where the Book's frown
> Sobers the sunlight? Who taught you to pray
> And scheme at once, your eyes turning
> Skyward, while your swift mind weighs
> Your heifer's chances in the next town's
> Fair on Thursday? Are your heart's coals
> Kindled for God, or is the burning
> Of your lean cheeks because you sit
> Too near that girl's smouldering gaze?
> Tell me, Davies, for the faint breeze
> From heaven freshens and I roll in it,
> Who taught you your deft poise?
>
> ('Chapel Deacon', p. 17)

He also knows full well of the harshness in people's dealings with each other which talk of God has to penetrate somehow. The farmer has not given his wife the attention she deserves:

> If you had spared from your long store
> Of days lavished upon the land
> But one for her where she lay fallow,
> Drying, hardening, withering to waste.
> But now – too late! You're an old tree,
> Your roots groping in her in vain.
>
> ('Age', p. 21)

Even after death the living can be haunted by the tyranny of those who have gone before them. The three sons whom we meet in a terrible family, to whom the poet introduces us, are dominated by their dead parents.

> John All and his lean wife,
> Whose forced complicity gave life
> To each loathed foetus, stare from the wall,
> Dead not absent. The night falls.
>
> ('Meet the Family'[2])

Given such facts, it is not surprising to find the poet's old impatience with the farmer re-emerging.

> Leave him, then, crazed and alone
> To pleach his dreams with his rough hands.
> Our ways have crossed and tend now apart;
> Ours to end in a field wisely sown,
> His in the mixen of his warped heart.
>   ('The Muck Farmer', p. 23)

Although such impatience is not surprising, what is surprising
and disturbing is the form it takes in some of the thoughts which
invade the poet–priest. He wishes to honour the country clergy:

> I see them working in old rectories
> By the sun's light, by candlelight,
> Venerable men, their black cloth
> A little dusty, a little green
> With holy mildew . . . .
>   ('The Country Clergy')

But then he is appalled to observe,

> And yet their skulls,
> Ripening over so many prayers,
> Toppled into the same grave
> With oafs and yokels.
>   (p. 28)

Moelwyn Merchant says, 'The central lines are shocking in their
direct expression of distinction in which few priests would dare
to think – much less articulate.'[3] The lines are indeed shocking,
but the possession of such thoughts is surely an occasion for
shame. It is not a case of 'not daring to think', but of the
difference between people in whom such thoughts find a home
and those in whom they do not. In so far as such thoughts do
invade the poet–priest, the poem is an honest record of them,
adding complexity to the details of his pilgrimage in verse.
Moelwyn Merchant, however, goes on to say, 'In its acceptance
of a cool uncharity, a mode of confession, of purgation, the poem
earns the right to its closing affirmation: "God in his time / Or out
of time will correct this"' (p. 28).[4] But is not the closing

affirmation of the same character as the supposed confession? Does it not darken the sentiments expressed even further? Not only do we find a priest saying' that he is superior to oafs and yokels and should not share their graves, but we also find him expressing the hope that God will recognise those truths through correction! But what is there to correct? Here is a conception of God who shares the priest's sense of class distinction in heaven; hardly the God who says that the first shall be last.[5]

Yet, despite the expression of such sentiments, more savage in their religious setting than any of the forms of impatience expressed hitherto, *Poetry for Supper* undoubtedly contains a maturing development in the relation between priest and peasant. There is an explicit reference to the relation when the poet asks Iago Prytherch for forgiveness because he realises that some of his readers will think that he has made him an object of fun.

> Made fun of you? That was their graceless
> Accusation, because I took
> Your rags for theme, because I showed them
> Your thought's bareness; science and art,
> The mind's furniture, having no chance
> To install themselves, because of the great
> Draught of nature sweeping the skull.
>
>   ('Iago Prytherch')

The priest's relation to the peasant has so many aspects that it cannot fall under a simple description.

> Fun? Pity? No word can describe
> My true feelings. I passed and saw you
> Labouring there, your dark figure
> Marring the simple geometry
> Of the square fields with its gaunt question.
> My poems were made in its long shadow
> Falling coldly across the page.
>
>   (p. 36)

It is in the shadow of the farmer that the poet–priest finds himself compelled to conduct his pilgrimage. The issues he has to face are determined by his relation to the farmer, so how can he be a figure of fun to him? So far removed would such a picture be from the whole truth that R. S. Thomas startles us with a poem where Prytherch is suddenly found in extremely unexpected company:

> You never heard of Kant, did you, Prytherch?
> A strange man! What would he have said
> Of your life here, free from the remote
> War of antimonies ; . . .
>
> ('Green Categories')

Kant, by pointing out what he thought were the limits of reason, thought that thereby room could be left for faith; that faith could come in at the right place. The possibility of faith is related to a sense of the moral law within, and to the presence of the starry heavens above. Whether Kant was right or not about this, R. S. Thomas sees that the same issue, in a radically different context, faces the peasant. How is faith to come in at the right place?

> Yet at night together
> In·your small garden, fenced from the wild moor's
> Constant aggression, you could have been at one,
> Sharing your faith over a star's blue fire.
>
> (p. 19)

In fact, if the priest compares himself with the peasant, he finds that, whereas he cannot deny the endurance shown in the peasant's life, he is often at a loss to know what has he to offer as a priest. Faced with the sufferings of his people, the priest despairs over the impotence of his language.

> Evans? Yes, many a time
> I came down his bare flight
> Of stairs into the gaunt kitchen
> With its wood fire, where crickets sang
> Accompaniment to the black kettle's
> Whine, and so into the cold
> Dark to smother in the thick tide
> Of night that drifted about the walls
> Of his stark farm on the hill ridge.

It was not the dark filling my eyes
And mouth appalled me; not even the drip
Of rain like blood from the one tree
Weather-tortured. It was the dark
Silting the veins of that sick man
I left stranded upon the vast
And lonely shore of his bleak bed.

('Evans'[6])

There should be words which he could offer to this man in his suffering, but he has none. So it may be to the end. The poet may have nothing to offer but songs which can do no more than express the failure of his own language.

Laid now on his smooth bed
For the last time, watching dully
Through heavy eyelids the day's colour
Widow the sky, what can he say
Worthy of record, the books all open,
Pens ready, the faces, sad,
Waiting gravely for the tired lips
To move once – what can he say?

His tongue wrestles to force one word
Past the thick phlegm; no speech, no phrases
For the day's news, just the one word 'sorry';
Sorry for the lies, for the long failure
In the poet's war; that he preferred
The easier rhythms of the heart
To the mind's scansion; that now he dies
Intestate, having nothing to leave
But a few songs, cold as stones
In the thin hands that asked for bread.

('Death of a Poet', p. 31)

And so the poet has good reason to ask for Prytherch's forgiveness. He says he has poured scorn on him 'From the cheap gallery of his mind'. He says of the farmer,

It was you who were right the whole time;
Right in this that the day's end

Find's you still in the same field
In which you started, your soul made strong
By the earth's incense, the wind's song.
                              ('Absolution')

Again, it seems that the only sense that endures is a sense of
endurance. But the poet–priest wants something more. How is
religious belief to transform the endurance? He is confronted by
Prytherch and, as before, sees his gestures in the field. He has
been pursued by the ambiguity of these gestures, but now the
poet sees them as gestures of forgiveness for his own incompe-
tence

                    to find
With the slow lifting up of your hand
No welcome, only forgiveness.
                              (p. 44)

The poet–priest, if he is to be true to his faith, must show how
praise has a bearing on the pleasant's plight. Yet, praise seems
foreign to his poetry at this stage. On the rare occasions it
appears, there is a desperation about it which robs it of a genuine
religious import. For example, when the poet tries to find some
measure of reassurance in 'The Cry', this is what happens:

Don't think it was all hate
That grew there; love grew there, too,
Climbing by small tendrils where
The warmth fell from the eyes' blue

Flame. Don't think even the dirt
And the brute ugliness reigned
Unchallenged. Among the fields
Sometimes the spirit, enchained

So long by the gross flesh, raised
Suddenly there its wild note of praise.
                              ('The Cry'[7])

The praise is wild, desperate. The title of the poem, after all, is not
'Praise', but 'The Cry'. Many of the causes of this desperation

in the priest–poet at this stage of his development have been
noted and are obvious enough. The most difficult thing to be
sure about is the nature of the hope which the poet finds
frustrated. Perhaps there is something amiss in the nature of the
hope itself. In face of the varied aspects of human life, there has
always been a deep desire among certain religious believers to
discover a pattern which will make sense of the whole. One of the
ways in which this has been done is to assume or postulate a
divine plan in which everything has its place. R. S. Thomas is
too honest and too perceptive a poet to be able to give assent to
such a notion of complete and final explanations. When he looks
at the facts that confront him, they are not facts which seem to
get their sense from an integrated whole. Hopes which are based
on or which long for such integration are therefore bound to be
frustrated.

> All through history
> The great brush has not rested,
> Nor the paint dried; yet what eye,
> Looking coolly, or, as we now,
> Through the tears' lenses, ever saw
> This work and it was not finished?
> ('The View from the Window'[8])

In face of these frustrations it is tempting simply to turn aside
from large questions. Indeed, it may be assumed that there is no
large sense to be found; there is simply the sense of this, that and
the other thing. Preoccupation with the private, or preoccupa-
tion with the form of poetry itself, becomes an end in itself. R. S.
Thomas regrets such developments:

> But what to do? Doctors in verse
> Being scarce now, most poets
> Are their own patients, compelled to treat
> Themselves first, their complaint being
> Peculiar always.
> ('The Cure')

He asks that the matter be reconsidered:

> Consider, you
> Whose rough hands manipulate

> The fine bones of a sick culture,
> What areas of that infirm body
> Depend solely on a poet's cure.[9]

What cure can R. S. Thomas mediate in his verse? We saw that, in *Song at the Year's Turning*, two poems, 'Pisces' and 'In a Country Church', particularly the latter, stood out from the rest in the conception of the religious task found in them. These poems, so far from wanting solutions to pain and suffering which consist in attempts to explain them away in terms of higher aims, attempt to mediate a sense of 'the higher' in religion by accepting the pain and suffering on their own terms. God becomes involved in the suffering and is no longer the external justification of it. I am not suggesting that either poem works out such a sense, but they show the direction in which the poet is endeavouring to move. In *Poetry for Supper* a poem, 'The Journey', similar in spirit, stands out from the rest. It faces squarely the different experiences, the fluctuating fortunes, a man will meet on his journey. First, there are those experiences which have dominated R. S. Thomas's poetry up to this point.

> And if you go up that way, you will meet with a man,
> Leading a horse, whose eyes declare:
> There is no God.
>
> ('The Journey')

But there are experiences of a better kind:

> Take no notice
> There will be other roads and other men
> With the same creed, whose lips yet utter
> Friendlier greeting, men who have learned
> To pack a little of the sun's light
> In their cold eyes, whose hands are waiting
> For your hand.

This is often how it is with us: the natural hope for the friendlier rather than the dark roads. Would it not be perverse if it were otherwise? Sometimes, religion itself is characterised as the best road to lead to a happy ending. Other conceptions of religion, however, do not depend on good days outnumbering bad days, but rather involve dying to the expectation that the former *should* outnumber the latter. In 'The Journey',[10] the poet seems to go beyond a conception of the good life which depends on favourable experiences on the roads one happens to be travelling on. The poet says, therefore, that we should not linger with the hope of good times:

> But do not linger
> A smile is payment; the road runs on
> With many turnings towards the tall
> Tree to which the believer is nailed.

There will be many twists and turns in the poetic journey R. S. Thomas will take, but during it more emphasis will be given to this need to die to the expectation for compensations in life. At this stage, however, what we witness in the poetry is a struggle for an adequate language in which the journey 'towards the tall / Tree to which the believer is nailed' can be expressed.

It is as well to emphasise again and again the many twists and turns in the poet's pilgrimage. It is those which dominate the two volumes *Tares* (1961) and *The Bread of Truth* (1964). Largely, this is because there is no way in which the poet can by-pass the challenges set for him by Iago Prytherch and his way of life.

> There are two hungers, hunger for bread
> And hunger of the uncouth soul
> For the light's grace. I have seen both,
> And chosen for an indulgent world's
> Ear the story of one whose hands
> Have bruised themselves on the locked doors
> Of life; whose heart, fuller than mine
> Of gulped tears, is the dark well
> From which to draw, drop by drop,
> The terrible poetry of his kind.
>   ('The Dark Well', p. 9[11])

The poetry of his kind must be a poetry of the terrible if it is to do justice to his situation. Given that fact, however, the problem is of how religion speaks to the terribleness of what is shown there.

The dilemma facing the poet is shown in the text for the volume: 'Didst not thou sow good seed in thy field? From whence, then, hath it tares?' (Matthew 13:27). Despite the tares in the life of Walter Llywarch, he longs for the religious message which is supposed to be a source of hope.

> School in the week, on Sunday chapel:
> Tales of a land fairer than this
> Were not so tall, for others had proved it
> Without the grave's passport, they sent
> The fruit home for ourselves to taste.
> ('Walter Llywarch'[12])

But what does tasting such fruit amount to? Given one conception of religion, it is almost as if the very presence of tares is to be denied. The ideal, given in the Godhead, is perfection's contemplation of itself. God listens to the music of the world with bated breath,

> . . . trying to be sure
> That what he heard was at one
> With his own score, that nothing,
>
> No casual improvisation
> Or sounding of a false chord,
> Troubled the deep peace.
>
> It was this way he adored
> With a god's ignorance of sin
> The self he had composed.
> ('The Conductor', p. 13)

What is to be the relation of this alleged divine harmony to the obvious disharmonies in the world? One attempt by R. S. Thomas to extend the analogy between God and the Conductor by reference to the Crucifixion does not work. The analogy between a performance by Kreisler, in which the poet was close enough to see the physical strain involved in his playing, and the crucifixion of Jesus is a false one. It has to falsify the facts in an effort to achieve an effect.

> So it must have been on Calvary
> In the fiercer light of the thorns' halo:
> The men standing by, and that one figure,
> The hands bleeding, the mind bruised but calm,
> Making such music as lives still.
> And no one daring to interrupt
> Because it was himself that he played
> And closer than all of them the God listened.
>   ('The Musician', p. 19)

The poet does want to identify God with the suffering, but how is
it to be done? It simply is not true that no one dared to interrupt
at the Cross 'Because it was himself that he played'. On the
contrary, he was reviled by the majority and the silence of the
believers was one of dismay; not of awe. It is in face of interrup-
tions such as these, and other interruptions to the hope for
harmony, such as those we have seen, that religious sense has to
be mediated. Further, in this volume, as in previous ones, it is
the challenge of the interruptions which threatens hopes of a
religious harmony. The poet is haunted by a priest's failure to
find a language adequate to meet them, as, for example, when he
visits on her ninetieth birthday a woman who dreams of a world
that has long ceased to exist:

> You bring her greeting
> And praise for having lasted so long
> With time's knife shaving the bone.
> Yet no bridge joins her own
> World with yours, all you can do
> Is lean kindly across the abyss
> To hear words that were once wise.
>   ('Ninetieth Birthday', p. 23)

As the farmer's world grows more prosperous, it is harder for the
priest to speak to him. With the increasing mechanisation on the
land, the farmer's own relationship with the land is changing.

> Can't you see
> Behind the smile on the times' face
> The cold brain of the machine

That will destroy you and your race?
> ('Too Late', p. 25)

The land's bleakness only testifies to the absence of God, and all
the poet can do is to pray that his heart is not hardened by all he
sees.

> I have looked it in the face.
> I have seen land emptied of Godhead,
> The wind blowing cold and the rain falling;
> Men going forth on slow tractors
> To turn the earth with hate in their hearts,
> Leaving behind them the farm's drudge,
> Breeder of children who have said No!
> To the spirit's usual invitation.
>
> How am I better than all these,
> Who have only the will to believe God
> Bleeds in the soil, the unloved body
> Their wheels mangle? Sweeten that will
> With grace, life, lest I grow hard
> Like them but for the wrong reason.
> > ('Earth', p. 46)

The danger of the deadening interruptions of life which threaten
to destroy belief in God is not only in the peasant. It threatens
the priest too. It threatens us all. But if it is to be overcome, it is
not by ignoring its challenges. Recognition of that fact is the
furthest point of the poetic journey in *Tares*.

> Yes, that's how I was,
> I know that face,
> That bony figure
> Without grace
> Of flesh or limb;
> In health happy,
> Careless of the claim
> Of the world's sick
> Or the world's poor;
> In pain craven -
> Lord, breathe once more

> On that sad mirror
> Let me be lost
> In mist for ever
> Rather than own
> Such bleak reflections.
> Let me go back
> On my two knees
> Slowly to undo
> The knot of life
> That was tied there.
>   ('Judgement Day'[13])

The heart of the matter, however, is to show in verse how such knots are untied by being on one's knees.

The struggle with the task of mediating a religious sense is not advanced very much in *The Bread of Truth*. The peasant's gestures still challenge him, and the poet–priest is acutely aware that they may amount to no more than an indication of his own misunderstandings.

> He was in the fields, when I set out.
> He was in the fields, when I came back.
> In between, what long hours,
> What centuries might have elapsed.
> Did he look up? His arm half
> Lifted was more to ward off
> My foolishness.
>   ('Truth', p. 38[14])

It is the hours between, even the centuries between, the priestly vocation and the harsh realities of life that worry the priest. The priest says of a tramp who comes to his door:

> He looks at his feet,
> I look at the sky;
>   ('Tramp', p. 23)

When he looks at some of the sinister scenes on the farm, he sees what religion has become for some:

There was Dai Puw. He was no good.
They put him in the fields to dock swedes,
And took the knife from him, when he came home
At late evening with a grin
Like the slash of a knife on his face.

There was Llew Puw, and he was no good.
Every evening after the ploughing
With the big tractor he would sit in his chair,
And stare into the tangled fire garden,
Opening his slow lips like a snail.

There was Huw Puw, too. What shall I say?
I have heard him whistling in the hedges
On and on, as though winter
Would never again leave those fields,
And all the trees were deformed.

And lastly there was the girl:
Beauty under some spell of the beast.
Her pale face was the lantern
By which they read in life's dark book
The shrill sentence: God is love.

('On the Farm'[15])

Moelwyn Merchant finds comfort here where I find none. He
says of the last verse: 'In all their bizarre half-perceptions, this is
not the first time that the men of the country have been re-
deemed by their womenkind, though here in another dimen-
sion.'[16] A. E. Dyson's verdict on the poem is more qualified,
but he still thinks that, on the whole, the closing lines offer a
redeeming sense. He believes the irony of the conclusion is 'held
in check by the archetypal image, 'Beauty under some spell of
the beast', and by the authenticity of the message the girl
conveys, despite the savage thrust of "shrill" '.[17] I find this poem
more sinister, because less explicit, than 'Meet the Family'. We
do not need to speculate explicitly about the girl to know her
fate. It ought not to be forgotten that beauty here *is* said to be
under some spell of the beast and that, when the sentence 'God is
love' comes, it *is* a shrill one.

Yet, despite all the difficulties and distortions, the poet–priest's struggle with the peasant's way of life goes on. He recognises his indebtedness to him.

> You served me well, Prytherch.
> From all my questionings and doubts;
>   ('Servant')

The poet recognises that truth, of course, is not confined to the context of his relationship with the peasant.

>   Not that you gave
> The whole answer. Is truth so bare,
> So dark, so dumb, as on your hearth
> And in your company I found it?

He realises too, however, that the other avenues of truth are not open to the peasant. But it is in the context of what is open to the peasant that the poet–priest seeks to mediate religious sense.

>   Not choice for you,
> But seed sown upon the thin
> Soil of a heart, not rich, nor fertile,
> Yet capable of the one crop,
> Which is the bread of truth that I break.
>   (p. 41)

It is clear that the peasant has become inseparable at this stage, from the nature and character of R. S. Thomas's poetic journey.

> He has become part of me,
> Aching in me like a bone
> Often bruised. Through him I learn
> Emptiness of the bare mind
> Without knowledge, and the frost
> Of knowledge, where there is no love.
>   ('He', p. 46)

The emptiness of the mind without knowledge reminds us of the poet's worry at the vacancy of the peasant's mind. Yet, knowledge itself has to be redeemed by love. But what kind of knowledge is required where religious sense is concerned? Is there a context in which understanding involves emptying the mind of what is often regarded as knowledge, and where love is a kind of dying to what we think we know? Knowing what is to come later in R. S. Thomas's development as a poet, the last lines of 'He' foreshadow some of the central issues the poet is to grapple with. But at this stage of the struggle for religious sense, characterised sometimes by repetition and slow progress, it is easy to conclude that, although 'R. S. Thomas does not think life in the Church clashes with his life as a poet', nevertheless, 'His poems, indeed, are on a superficial level overwhelmingly secular, although there are a few where there is a near mystical sense of the love of God.'[18] That conclusion does not work hard enough for clarity. There is an uneasy tension between calling a view 'superficial' and calling it 'overwhelming' at the same time. We have seen that the so-called secular poems are nothing less than the necessary context in which a hard-won religious sense has to emerge. The 'near mystical sense of the love of God' would mean little without them. On the one hand, we need to recognise that, in relation to what he sees about him, 'When dealing with these subjects, there is a continued refusal to be deceived or too easily comforted: it is a poetry without illusion.'[19] On the other hand, this honesty serves a wider search: it 'is entirely obvious to anybody who already knows R. S. Thomas's work: . . . that the argument is approached, must be approached, from the position and function of a priest in the Church in Wales.'[20] To forget that would be to misunderstand the path already traversed and the nature of the journey in verse which is yet to come.

5   Waiting for God

In the volumes *Pietà* (1966) and *Not that he Brought Flowers* (1968), there is a further development in the poet's attempt to mediate religious sense. In particular, the question of how God speaks to the diverse character of human life becomes far more central then it has been hitherto.

In *Pietà* the poet's expression of praise of God seems ironic. The problem is that the praise seems to be offered because the will of God appears to be consistent with anything that happens in the world. It is said that the world is governed by divine providence. It might even be said that things go according to God's plan. The difficulty is in understanding what this means. If a drama is being acted out according to an author's script, then, if the action in the drama departs from the script, this can be pointed out by reference to it. To make such a discovery, there must be a distinction between action and the script. It is just this distinction that is missing in the notion of divine providence. How is one to know when anything that happens is a departure from the divine script, since everything that happens is supposed to be in accordance with it? The conclusion seems to be that the notion of a plan or a script, when applied to God, is an idle wheel. Against such a background, the poet's admiration for God's apparent acceptance of all things is bound to appear ironic. In 'Because' it may well be that the poet wants to work through to a conception of divine judgement which is necessarily different from our own, but this is not to be achieved by a suspension of moral judgements involving common decency. It is certainly premature to see this poem in terms of a triumph which consists of 'the ability to praise a God who sees and judges not as we judge'.[1] The poem, since it does not advance this alternative sense, is more akin to a reminder of an issue not to be ducked.

I praise you because
I envy your ability to
See these things: the blind hands
Of the aged combing sunlight
For pity; the starved fox and
The obese pet; the way the world
Digests itself and the thin flame
Scours. The youth enters
The brothel, and the girl enters
The nunnery, and a bell tolls.
Viruses invade the blood.
On the smudged empires the dust
Lies and in the libraries
Of the poets. The flowers wither
On love's grave. This is what
Life is, and on it your eye
Sets tearless, and the dark
Is dear to you as the light.
                    ('Because', p. 8²)

It is not hard to see the suppressed questions in the poet's 'praise'. Should any eye, including the eye of God, be tearless when it looks on such a scene? The poet obviously wants to put this consideration before God, but when he does so, no satisfactory answer seems to be forthcoming. Instead of an answer he is told simply to accept. But should the mind accept any more than the eye be tearless?

And God said: How do you know?
And I went out into the fields
At morning and it was true.

Nothing denied it, neither the bowed man
On his knees, nor the animals,
Nor the birds notched on the sky's

Surface. His heart was broken
Far back, and the beasts yawned
Their boredom. Under the song

> Of the larks, I heard the wheels turn
> Rustily. But the scene held;
> The cold landscape returned my stare;
>
> There was no answer. Accept; accept.
> And under the green capitals,
> The molecules and the blood's virus.
>
> ('Amen', p. 15)

Inevitably, questions form in the mind of the priest. Should everything be accepted? Are there not some things to be grateful for and others to protest against? On that distinction does not any decent ethics take its stand? And what of the readiness to thank for the precious little instead of protesting against the little that it is? Is this something the priest should allow to go unquestioned? Yet, seeing, it, he does not intervene. Why not?

> What is a man's
> Price? For promises of a break
> In the clouds; for harvests that are not all
> Wasted; for one animal born
> Healthy, where seven have died,
> He will kneel down and give thanks
> In a chapel whose stones are wrenched
> From the moorland.
>   I have watched them bent
> For hours over their trade,
> Speechless, and have held my tongue
> From its question. It was not my part
> To show them, like a meddler from the town,
> Their picture, nor the audiences
> That look at them in pity or pride.
>
> ('There'[3])

The reaction of many would be that the suppressed question should break out as a rage against the grotesque assumption that all this suffering is *for* something. What is one to think of a god who is conceived of as the author of such a cruel obstacle race? Should not all we know lead us to protest along with Mark and Matthew Puw:

Mark Puw: Who put me here?
                I must get on with this job;
                The rain is coming. I must get on
                With this job. Who put me
                Here? The bugger; I'd like
                To see him now in my place.
Mathew Puw: There are times
                When I could wreck the whole bloody
                Farm. Pig music, sheep music, the grey
                Traffic of the clouds going by
                I could get shut of the lot,
                If it wasn't for him and Mair.
                                    ('Gospel Truth', p. 32)

What god comes in such a context? The poet–priest is torn
between what land and sea tell him and the answers he finds in
his theological texts. Is there any reconciliation between the
lessons of the books and the lessons of nature? The poet–priest
is unsure:

                    Between their pages
        The beast sleeps and never looks out
        Through the print's bars. Have I been wise
        In the past, letting my nostrils
        Plan my day? That salt scrubbing
        Left me unclean. Am I wise now,
        With all this pain in the air,
        To keep my room, reading perhaps
        Of that Being whose will is our peace?
                        ('Within Sound of the Sea', p. 13)

But how can there be an adequate conception of God's will
which will bring peace with all the pain in the air? Is it not better
to give up craving for a sense other than a sense of endurance?
The latter is by no means to be identified with craven resigna-
tion. It has a nobility and a grandeur of its own which the poet
recognises and is eager to celebrate. He finds it easy to call it to
mind:

        He is never absent, but like a slave
        Answers to the mind's bidding,

Endlessly ploughing, as though autumn
Were the one season he knew.
Sometimes he pauses to look down
To the grey farmhouse, but no signals
Cheer him; there is no applause
For his long wrestling with the angel
Of no name. I can see his eye
That expects nothing, that has the rain's
Colourlessness. His hands are broken
But not his spirit. He is like bark
Weathering on the tree of his kind.

He will go on; that much is certain.
Beneath him tenancies of the fields
Will change; machinery turn
All to noise. But on the walls
Of the mind's gallery that face
With the hills framing it will hang
Unglorified, but stern like the soil.

('The Face'[4])

The celebration of the peasant's powers of endurance constitutes
a challenge to religion. We have R. S. Thomas's own testimony
to this effect:

Well, I came out of a kind of bourgeois environment which,
especially in modern times, is protected; it's cushioned from
some of the harsher realities; and this muck and blood and
hardness, the rain and the spittle and the phlegm of farm life
was, of course, a shock to begin with and one felt that this was
something not quite part of the order of things. But, as one
experienced it and saw how definitely part of their lives this
was, sympathy grew in oneself and compassion and admira-
tion; and since you've got in these communities people who've
probably been like this over the centuries, the very fact that
they endure at all – that they make a go of it at all – suggests
that they have got some hard core within them. One has to
face this as a priest, this sort of attack, as it were, from their
side.[5]

In face of people and a life such as this, what cheering signals come from the direction of religion? Given certain conceptions of religion, the honest answer is that there are none. The poet–priest wrestling with such conceptions is prepared to admit as much. When he conducts his services he often feels that the words on offer have no purchase.

> We stand looking at
> Each other. I take the word 'prayer'
> And present it to them. I wait idly,
> Wondering what their lips will
> Make of it. But they hand back
> Such presents. I am left alone
> With no echoes to the amen
> I dreamed of. I am saved by music
> From the emptiness of this place
> Of despair. As the melody rises
> From nothing, their mouths take up the tune,
> And the roof listens. I call on God
> In the after silence, and my shadow
> Wrestles with him upon a wall
> Of plaster, that has all the nation's
> Hardness in it. They see me thrown
> Without movement of their oblique eyes.
>   ('Service', p. 36)

The reason why the poet is able to celebrate the peasant's endurance, show us his cries of despair, is that that despair is not to be found only in the peasant's experience. There are moments when the same despair consumes the priest too. It is not only the Puw brothers who ask what their lives amount to and who grapple in vain to find sense and purpose there.

> Someone must have thought of putting me here;
> It wasn't myself did it.
> What do I find to my taste?
> Annually the grass comes up green;
> The earth keeps in rotary motion.
> There is loveliness growing, where might have been truth's
> Bitter berries. The reason tempers
> Most of the heart's stormier moods.

But there's an underlying despair
Of what should be most certain in my life:
This hard image that is reflected
In mirrors and in the eyes of friends.
It is for this that the air comes in thin
At the nostril, and dries to a crust.

('Who?', p. 39)

Faced with such harsh facts, in nature despite its loveliness, and in one's own life, the religious message may seem to be nothing more than a hard, cruel joke.

I have seen it standing up grey,
Gaunt, as though no sunlight
Could ever thaw out the music
Of its great bell; terrible
In its own way, for religion
Is like that. There are times
When a black frost is upon
One's whole being, and the heart
In its bone belfry hangs and is dumb.

('The Belfry')

Yet, even if no clear sense may have emerged for him, the struggle to mediate such sense continues. The priest is not prepared to declare the struggle over:

But who is to know? Always,
Even in winter in the cold
Of a stone church, on his knees
Someone is praying, whose prayers fall
Steadily through the hard spell
Of weather that is between God
And himself. Perhaps they are warm rain
That brings the sun and afterwards flowers
On the raw graves and throbbing of bells.[6]

This tentativeness will never disappear entirely from R. S. Thomas's poetry. It is itself an aspect of his struggle for an adequate language of faith. But, as volume succeeds volume, so we see the poet, more frequently, wait on a God who is different

from the god who is the provider of unlikely and even seedy
explanations of the world's ills. In the present volume, for
example, the enduring prayers he mentions with such tentative-
ness in 'The Belfry' are meant to introduce us and himself slowly
to a conception of patience which goes beyond resolute endur-
ance, however magnificent. The notion of patience involved
takes us beyond resignation too and it is to be found, for
example, in reflections on natural scenes. Here is the hope of
grace in nature which goes beyond natural grace. Looking at
gliding swifts in the sky, the poet concludes that 'There is no
solving the problem they pose'. But, then, he goes beyond seeing
their movements under the aspect of a problem to be solved.

> Sometimes they meet
> In the high air; what is engendered
> At contact? I am learning to bring
> Only my wonder to the contemplation
> Of the geometry of their dark wings.
>   ('Swifts', p. 9)

Wonders are not explanations. This is not a case of wondering
whether or why, but a wondering at. In this context the wonders
are to be fed on, not explained.

The patience which is not unconnected with wonder is found
in the peasant too, but it has to be worked at.

> Take heart, Prytherch.
> Over yon the planets stand,
> And have seen more ills than yours.
> This canker was in the bone
> Before man bent to his image
> In the pool's glass. Violence has been
> And will be again. Between better
> And worse is no bad place.
>
> For a labourer, whose lot is to seem
> Stationary in traffic so fast.
> Turn aside, I said; do not turn back,
> There is no forward and no back
> In the fields, only the year's two
> Solstices, and patience between.
>   ('Aside'[7])

The task for the poet–priest is to show the sense patience can have in the context of religious faith. Patience involves dying to certain expectations which the poet has entertained as God's questioner and which he will entertain again. These expectations are expectations for answers; answers, explanations and justifications which will show why everything happens in just the way it does. The poet's frustrations have come from the fact that in asking these questions, all he has been confronted by is silence. Silence has been often the barrier between himself and faith. What he is realising slowly and with difficulty is that silence of that kind may be a precondition of faith rather than an obstacle to it. It may not be too much of an exaggeration to say that the nature of men's religious faith may be determined by looking at their attitude to the silence which confronts human questioning of the way things are.

> Often I try
> To analyse the quality
> Of its silences. Is this where God hides
> From my searching? I have stopped to listen,
> After the few people have gone,
> To the air recomposing itself
> For vigil. It has waited like this
> Since the stones grouped themselves about it.
> These are the hard ribs
> Of a body that our prayers have failed
> To animate. Shadows advance
> From their corners to take possession
> Of places the light held
> For an hour. The bats resume
> Their business. The uneasiness of the pews
> Ceases. There is no other sound
> In the darkness but the sound of a man
> Breathing, testing his faith
> On emptiness, nailing his questions
> One by one to an untenanted cross.
>
>   ('In Church'[8])

We have already noted in previous volumes that religious steps forward are found in poems such as 'Pisces', 'In a Country Church' and 'The Journey'. Those steps continue in a handful of poems in the present collection: 'In Church', 'Ah!', 'Pietà' and

'The Moor'. In the poem quoted above we can see that the poet–priest has to die to his old questions. It is only by dying to the old questions that wonder can come in at the right place. But this act of dying is not easy to achieve. It is always tempting to think that silence, our inability to find answers, happens to hide God from us. Faith, on this view, lasts while ignorance lasts. There is an ignorance of another kind, however, which finds an answer in a use of the actual silence. Alternatively, this acceptance of silence is resisted by attempting to make God more congenially understandable to us. But, as Simone Weil says, if we understood God he would be less than ourselves.

> There's no getting round it,
> It's a hell of a thing, he said, and looked grave
> To prove it. What he said was
> The truth. I would make different
> Provision; for such flesh arrange
> Exits down less fiery paths. But the God
> We worship fashions the world
> From such torment, and every creature
> Decorates it with its tribute of blood.
>
> ('Ah!', p. 45)

The attempt to penetrate the silence, to find answers, makes finding a point in things central. Silence, on such a view, is an obstacle to faith because no point is forthcoming. The silence of God with which the poet struggles is one which starts from not finding a point in all things. Leaving things to God involves ceasing to see events as partial with respect to oneself. The will of God is, in an important sense, indifferent and impartial – his rain falls on the just and the unjust. The impartiality of the rain makes it possible for it to be seen as a gift, as an act of grace freely bestowed. Such a realisation comes to the poet on the quiet moor which is like a church to him.

> There were no prayers said. But stillness
> Of the heart's passions – that was praise
> Enough; and the mind's cession
> Of its kingdom. I walked on,
> Simple and poor, while the air crumbled
> And broke on me generously as bread.
>
> ('The Moor'[9])

But is the torment and suffering of the world to be seen as the will of God too? The poet–priest realises that acceptance of silence is necessary in this context too. The sense of God's grace must be mediated through suffering and compassion. If either is ignored, God turns out to be a monster. Such mediation is expressed in 'Pietà', but its significance in the kinds of situation we have encountered in R. S. Thomas's poems will continue to determine the prevailing content of the poetic struggle to come. Due attention will have to be given to a necessary compassion in face of suffering with its imperative to remove it, but due attention will have to be paid too to the fact that some suffering is necessary, defying all efforts at elimination.

> Always the same hills
> Crowd the horizon,
> Remote witnesses
> Of the still scene.
>
> And in the foreground
> The tall Cross,
> Sombre, untenanted,
> Aches for the Body
> That is back in the cradle
> Of a maid's arms.
> ('Pietà'[10])

There must always be room for those who cradle the sufferings of the world. But even that compassion has to be informed by the stark truth that at the centre of Christianity there may have to be an embracing of a cross.

The extent of the task facing the poet in his efforts to mediate a religious sense is seen in the volume *Not that he Brought Flowers*. How is the religious acceptance of all things from God different from bland indifference, an uncaring neutrality? What if what seems to be the love of God is simply a failure to face this neutral indifference?

> It will always win.
> Other men will come as I have

To stand here and beat upon it
As on a door, and ask for love,
For compassion, for hatred even; for anything
Rather than this blank indifference,
Than the neutrality of its answers, if they can be called
   answers
These grey skies, these wet fields,
With the wind's winding-sheet upon them.

('That'[11])

In this volume it is the difficulties of the priest which predominate. It is the first volume in which Prytherch does not appear. If mediation of sense there is to be, it must be a mediation which does not circumvent the afflictions men have to undergo. These afflictions are sometimes sufficient to stop the songs in their hearts.

And one said, This man can sing;
Let's listen to him. But the other,
Dirt on his mind, said, No, let's
Queer him. And the first, being weak,
Consented. So the Thing came
Nearer him, and its breath caused
Him to retch, and none knew why.
But he rested for one long month,
And after began to sing
For gladness, and the Thing stood,
Letting him, for a year, for two;
Then put out its raw hand
And touched him, and the wound took
Over, and the nurses wiped off
The poetry from his cracked lips.

('No'[12])

This is what religion has to speak to. R. S. Thomas refuses to etherealise faith. It must speak to austere conditions, to the two cronies of whom we are told,

Mildew and pus and decay
They deal in, and feed on mucous
And wind, diet of a wet land.

('Look')

The poet concludes with the insistence:

> We must dip belief
> Not in dew nor in the cool fountain
> Of beech buds, but in seas
> Of manure through which they squelch
> To the bleakness of their assignations.[13]

The poet is not prepared to accept, uncritically, the answers of those philosophers who try to explain evil away in terms of a wider divine plan.

> I know all the tropes
> Of religion, how God is not there
> To go to; how time is what we buy
> With his absence, and how we look
> Through the near end of the binocular at pain,
> Evil, deformity. I have tried
> Bandaging my sharp eyes
> With humility, but still the hearing
> Of the ear holds; from far off as Tibet
> The cries come.
>
> ('After the Lecture')

Anthony Conran has said of this poem that 'the metaphysical and theological problem of pain is presented as one of those puzzled questioners who come up after a public lecture, and diffidently ask the one question it is always impossible to answer'.[14] It is important to remember, however, that the question remains unanswerable only if we accept the premiss from which it is asked. Perhaps what is needed is not an answer to the question, but a way of ceasing to ask it by working through it. This is the task R. S. Thomas sees himself confronted with:

> From one not to be penned
> In a concept, and differing in kind
> From the human; whose attributes are the negations
> Of thought; who holds us at bay with
> His symbols, the opposed emblems
> Of hawk and dove, what can my prayers win

For the kindred, souls brought to the bone
To be tortured, and burning, burning
Through history with their own strange light?[15]

Again and again, the poet–priest wants to make it his task to
put these austere conditions before God. He verges on being a
protestor; he insists on being a mediator.

> Daily I take their side
> In their quarrel, calling their faults
> Mine. How do I serve so
> This being they have shut out
> Of their houses, their thoughts, their lives?
>
> ('They', p. 39[16])

He asks his flock under the burden of singing of their woes,

> What do you want of me?
> I am here and answer
> To my name. I rise, work,
> And keep my lusts
> To myself. Through tattered sunlight
> I go, and make your dreams
> Mine.
>
> ('Please'[17])

The priest is also confronted by those with no ill will in them to
whom his words mean nothing:

> A simple man,
> He liked the crease on the water
> His cast made, but had no pity
> For the broken backbone
> Of water or fish.
>
> One of his pleasures, thirsty,
> Was to ask a drink
> At the hot farms;
> Leaving with a casual thank you,
> As though they owed it him.

I could have told of the living water
That springs pure.
He would have smiled then,
Dancing his speckled fly in the shallows,
Not understanding.
('The Fisherman'[18])

It is true that the priest knows of religious saints, such as Saint Julian, who embrace the leper whom others shun,

contaminating
Himself with a kiss,
With the love that
Our science has disinfected.
('St Julian and the Leper'[19])

On the other hand, he has to admit that even worship in the eucharist is often characterised by an ambivalence which he cannot ignore.

The people rise
And walk to the churches'
Stone lanterns, there to kneel
And eat the new bread
Of love, washing it down
With the sharp taste
Of blood they will shed.
('Christmas'[20])

Faced with such austerities, lack of understanding, ambivalences and far-off saintly ideals, the priest's exercise of his ministry is itself a stumbling affair. But would the poet–priest turn his back on his calling for that reason?

'Crippled soul', do you say? looking at him
From the mind's height; 'limping through life
On his prayers. There are other people
In the world, sitting at table
Contented, though the broken body
And the shed blood are not on the menu'.

'Let it be so', I say. 'Amen and amen'.
('The Priest'[21])

And so we see the priest at

> Moments of great calm
> Kneeling before an altar
> Of wood in a stone church
> In summer, waiting for the God
> To speak . . . .

This may be thought to be a return to that cluster of poems in which the poet makes advances in his conception of waiting on God, but it is not so. There is too much hesitation and ambivalence in the sentiments which come to the surface.

> Prompt me, God;
> But not yet. When I speak,
> Though it be you who speak
> Through me, something is lost.
> The meaning is in the waiting.
> ('Kneeling'[22])

Various echoes come in these words. If the last line were unmodified, the reference would be to the waiting on God which is a form of patience and dying to the request for a justification of God's ways to men. But the last line is modified by those which precede it. The 'Prompt me, God; but not yet' is a clear echo of St Augustine's, 'Save me, God; but not yet.' There is still something in the poet which draws back from the religious sense which threatens to emerge. His utterances, even when prompted by God, are inadequate. So the waiting which is the meaning is still a waiting in the tension which is created by all the various pressures we have observed. So, even with the religious insights the poet has achieved, there are still moments, such as this, when the waiting for God is all, even though the outcome is uncertain. It is highly misleading to make such moments the essence of faith, as the following remarks would do: 'The test of faith ultimately is the will to maintain indefinitely a state of suspense. The "meaning" for us is the attainment of this perfection of anticipation in which God might come.'[23] This meaning is the meaning which a *test* of faith has. It is not the only aspect of faith, far less its essence. The important point is that when one has to wait, one has to realise that God cannot be taken by storm. As R. S. Thomas has said,

> God, reality, whatever it is, is not going to be forced, it's not going to be put to question, it works in its own time. I suppose one projected this image of oneself kneeling, either entering a moorland, a lonely bare moorland, or entering the village church and just waiting; waiting but nothing happening. And out of this, of course, comes the feeling that perhaps this is all one is required to do. It's the Milton idea, isn't it, that they also serve who only stand and wait?[24]

But Milton says, 'they *also* serve', to indicate that this is one situation among many. Sometimes we have to wait for God, which, of course, is not a matter of 'hanging around'. We must not be misled by the poet's reference to 'nothing happening'. The whole context in which he waits has to be kept in mind if that nonsensical conclusion is to be avoided.[25] The poet waits for God. But not all forms of waiting on God are a waiting for God. There is a danger of running these together; a danger which then leads to the confused and contradictory conclusion that if God comes to a person faith is lost! 'If and when he does come this patient readiness which is faith is lost.'[26] Waiting on God is the paradigm of faith; waiting for God is one aspect of that faith. In 'Kneeling' it is that aspect which emerges.

6   God's Reflections

The volume *H'm* (1972) marks a major step forward in R. S. Thomas's poetic pilgrimage. Referring to this volume, and the further two volumes of the seventies, A. E. Dyson says, rightly, 'If we had Thomas's poetry to this point alone, he would still rank among the truly important moderns. But it is the three volumes of the 1970s . . . which take him into a still rarer class of excellence.'[1] Gone is all trace of a romanticism about the countryside, the bland philosophy which assumes that a mediation of sense is unnecessary, that natural surroundings will automatically convey meaning. The most forceful dismissal of such romanticism is delivered, in fact, in *Young and Old* (1972), which contains poems which feature startlingly, to say the least, in the Chatto Poets for the Young series.

> About living in the country?
> I yawn; that step, for instance –
> No need to look up – Evans
> On his way to the fields, where he hoes
> Up one row of mangolds and down
> The next one. You needn't wonder
> What goes on in his mind, there is nothing
> Going on there; the unemployment
> Of the lobes is established. His small dole
> Is kindness of the passers-by
> Who mister him, who read an answer
> To problems in the way his speech
> Comes haltingly, and his eyes reflect
> Stillness. I would say to them
> About living in the country, peace
> Can deafen one, beauty surprise
> No longer. There is only the thud
> Of the slow foot up the long lane
> At morning and back at night.
>
> ('The Country'[2])

As we saw in the last chapter, the poet is struggling with a
language which will allow talk of God to come in at the right
place. But what kind of God is to come? The answers we want to
give to this question are still the main source of the tensions we
find in *H'm*. On the one hand, there is a desire for the God of
theodicies, the God of explanation and justification; the God
who has reasons for the way things go. R. S. Thomas shows what
such a conception of God has to answer for. If God is to be
thought of as an agent among agents, only infinitely more
powerful than his fellow agents, what are we to make of him? No
religious syntax can be satisfactory which depends on such a
falsification of the facts. Above all, the facts he does not want to
avoid are those of the sufferings to which human beings are
subject. There can be no contrast of such sufferings with a
benign world of nature. Against any attempt to find a neat
optimistic picture of order in nature we have the eloquently
expressed protest of Hume's Philo:

> Look around this universe. What an immense profusion of
> beings, animated and organized, sensible and active! You
> admire this prodigious variety and fecundity. But inspect a
> little more narrowly these living existences, the only beings
> worth regarding. How hostile and destructive to each other!
> How insufficient all of them for their own happiness! How
> contemptible or odious to the spectator! The whole presents
> nothing but the idea of a blind nature, impregnated by a great
> vivifying principle, and pouring forth from her lap, without
> discernment or parental care, her maimed and abortive
> children.[3]

But is there any more reason to speak of discernment or parental
care if we try to attribute such qualities to God based on
inferences from what happens to men? R. S. Thomas provides a
savage rejection of such hopes. He shows us what kind of god
would emerge from such arguments:

> And God said, I will build a church here
> And cause this people to worship me,
> And afflict them with poverty and sickness
> In return for centuries of hard work
> And patience. And its walls shall be hard as

Their hearts, and its windows let in the light
Grudgingly, as their minds do, and the priest's words be
  drowned
By the wind's caterwauling. All this I will do,

Said God, and watch the bitterness in their eyes
Grow, and their lips suppurate with
Their prayers. And their women shall bring forth
On my altars, and I will choose the best
Of them to be thrown back into the sea.

And that was only on one island.

('The Island', p. 26[4])

The priest wishes it were otherwise, that there should be a harmony evident to the beholder, but it is not to be.

And I standing in the shade
Have seen it a thousand times
Happen: first theft, then murder;
Rape; the rueful acts
Of the blind hand. I have said
New prayers, or said the old
In a new way. Seeking the poem
In the pain, I have learned
Silence is best, paying for it
With my conscience. I am eyes
Merely, witnessing virtue's
Defeat; seeing the young born
Fair, knowing the cancer
Awaits them. One thing I have asked
Of the disposer of the issues
Of life: that truth should defer
To beauty. It was not granted.

('Petition', p. 12)

The request is not granted. But should the request be made in the first place? Without doubt, the request is natural enough; it is a cry from the midst of affliction. There can be no genuine religious faith which does not work through the question. But is it to be worked out on its own terms? The poet–priest shows

what happens if one proceeds on the assumption that it has to
be. The priest has to learn that if he seeks a harmonising poem in
the pain, he is reduced to silence. But should he be silent?
Doesn't one have to betray one's conscience to keep silent in
such circumstances? Surely, the poet must admit that, given
these terms of reference, the poem asked for must die on his lips.

> And the dogfish, spotted like God's face,
> Looks at him, and the seal's eye-
> Ball is cold. Autumn arrives
> With birds rattling in brown showers
> From hard skies. He holds out his two
> Hands, calloused with the long failure
> Of prayer: Take my life, he says
> To the bleak sea, but the sea rejects him
> Like wrack. He dungs the earth with
> His children and the earth yields him
> Its stone. Nothing he does, nothing he
> Says is accepted, and the thin dribble
> Of his poetry dries on the rocks
> Of a harsh landscape under an ailing sun.
>
> ('He'[5])

Slowly, surely, the poet's reflections begin to frame an accusa-
tion at the heavens. Perhaps the fault is not the poet's. Perhaps
the mistake is in thinking that there is a God who has sovereign
control of his creation. Perhaps there is no divine order behind
the veil. What if there is a radical disorder at the heart of things?
Is there not just as much reason to speak of disorder as there is to
speak of order? So speculated Hume's Philo:

> The world, for ought he knows, is very faulty and imperfect,
> compared to a superior standard; and was only the first rude
> essay of some infant Deity, who afterwards abandoned it,
> ashamed of his lame performance; it is the work only of some
> dependent, inferior Deity; and is the object of derision to his
> superiors: it is the production of old age and dotage in some
> superannuated Deity; and ever since his death, has run on at
> adventures, from the first impulse and active force, which it
> received from him . . . . I cannot, for my part, think, that so wild
> and unsettled a system of theology is, in any respect, prefer-
> able to none at all.[6]

The poet–priest does not let theology go entirely, as Philo advocates, but he does reject certain apologetic efforts at systematisation within it. He acknowledges that theology may be in a wild and unsettled state in its attempt to make a system out of the sense of things. In his poetry the acknowledgement takes the form of depicting a bewilderment in the Godhead itself. In R. S. Thomas we find a neat reversal of the emphasis found in the Argument from Design. In the argument it is God who can be inferred from an order we see about us. Order in life and nature is the ground on which we can infer a divine order. But in R. S. Thomas's poetry, life and nature are out of control, so failing to tell of God.

It was perfect. He could do
Nothing about it. Its waters
Were as clear as his own eye. The grass
Was his breath. The mystery
Of the dark earth was what went on
In himself. He loved and
Hated it with a parent's
Conceit, admiring his own
Work, resenting its
Independence. There were trysts
In the greenwood at which
He was not welcome. Youths and girls,
Fondling the pages of
A strange book, awakened
His envy. The mind achieved
What the heart could not. He began planning
The destruction of the long peace
Of the place. The machine appeared
In the distance, singing to itself
Of money. Its song was the web
They were caught in, men and women
Together. The villages were as flies
To be sucked empty.
             God secreted
A tear. Enough, enough,
He commanded, but the machine
Looked at him and went on singing.
                      ('Other', p. 37)

The world of the machine, with its promise of progress and profit, takes men further and further away from God, so much so that it can no longer show the sense of God's handiwork that a theology of explanation and justification seeks to find there.

> Machines were invented
> To cope, but they also were limited
> By our expectations.

The result, perhaps, could have been foreseen:

> Fortunes were made
> On the ability to disappoint.
>   ('Remedies', p. 29)

The machine can give no answer to the void created by what it destroys. In such a situation, the poet's task of mediating an alternative sense or of maintaining a threatened sense in verse is made all the more difficult. Material improvement was achieved at a high price:

> As life improved, their poems
> Grew sadder and sadder. Was there oil
> For the machine? It was
> The vinegar in the poet's cup.
>
> The tins marched to the music
> Of the conveyer belt. A billion
> Mouths opened. Production,
> Production, the wheels
>
> Whistled. Among the forests
> Of metal the one human
> Sound was the lament of
> The poets for deciduous language.
>   ('Postscript', p. 27)

This, then, is the graveyard of theodicies. The poet depicts God himself declaring such enterprises fruitless. In the poem below, however, an ambiguity still lurks. We do not see yet an outright rejection of the desire for the order which theodicies seek to impose. What we are told is that the God who seeks such an order has to admit that the hope for it is frustrated.

> And God thought: Pray away,
> Creatures; I'm going to destroy
> It. The mistake's mine,
> If you like. I have blundered
> Before; the glaciers erased
> My error.
>   I saw them go
> Further than you – palaces,
> Missiles. My privacy
> Was invaded; then the flaw
> Took over; they allied themselves
> With the dust. Winds blew away
> Their pasture. Their bones signalled
> From the desert to me
> In vain.
>   After the dust, fire;
> The earth burned. I have forgotten
> How long, but the fierce writing
> Seduced me. I blew with my cool
> Breath; the vapour condensed
> In the hollows. The sun was torn
> From my side. Out of the waters
> You came, as subtle
> As water, with your mineral
> Poetry and promises
> Of obedience. I listened to you
> Too long. Within the churches
> You built me you genuflected
> To the machine. Where will it
> Take you from the invisible
> Viruses, the personnel
> Of the darkness that do my will?
>   ('Soliloquy', p. 32)

So far from endorsing the hopes for a theodicy, God's dealings with man are represented simply as a series of whims, seductions and succumbings to caprice. As God withdraws from the results, where does that leave man?

The idiot goes round and around
With his brother in a bumping-car
At the fair. The famous idiot
Smile hangs over the car's edge,
Illuminating nothing. This is mankind
Being taken for a ride by a rich
Relation. The responses are fixed:
Bump, smile; bump, smile. And the current

Is generated by the smooth flow
Of the shillings. This is an orchestra
Of steel with the constant percussion
Of laughter. But where he should be laughing
Too, his features are split open, and look!
Out of the cracks come warm, human tears.

('The Fair', p. 38)

The poem brings us full circle to the only reaction which seems
to remain when the God of theodicies becomes hidden from
view. But this natural reaction is not enough for a poet–priest
who wants to achieve, as best he can, a religious syntax in verse.
He cannot return to this former concerns:

Come
Back to the rain and manure
Of Siloh, to the small talk,
Of the wind, and the chapel's
Temptation . . . .

(Invitation)

But neither can he put aside, as many poets have done, the large
questions posed by the possibility of religious belief. Certainly,
he cannot give in to the other invitation he hears:

Come

To the streets, where the pound
Sings . . . .

The poet is faithful to his calling:

> And I stay
> Here, listening to them, blowing
> On the small soul in my
> Keeping with such breath as I have.[7]

There is no turning–back for men and women. Their faith, if they are to have any, has to be refined in face of what awaits them. Echoing Milton's Adam and Eve, R. S. Thomas's Adam with his Eve faces what God has in store for him:

> I took your hand,
> Remembering you, and together,
> Confederates of the natural day,
> We went forth to meet the Machine.
> ('Once', p. 11)

What kind of meeting can there be which can let an authentic faith come in at the right place? The poems in *H'm* still to be discussed give a remarkable answer to this question. As Brian Morris has said, 'The poems of the four . . . volumes *H'm* (1972), *Laboratories of the Spirit* (1975), *The Way of It* (1977), and *Frequencies* (1978), are dominantly concerned with the quest for the *deus absconditus*, a search which takes the poet into new realms of science, philosophy, and theological speculation.'[8]

The very first characteristic of the songs the poet is about to give us is their explicit rejection of the premises which led the search for harmonising theodicies into such difficulties. The poet turns his back on the kind of religious impulses which seek to explain away the torment and suffering in the world. The poet insists that such facts must be embraced rather than ignored. But, of course, more than that is needed to take us beyond natural compassion for human endurance. The poet shows us a religious faith which actually depends on embracing the mixed character of human life in a way which does not deny its character. If a use can be found in suffering, it is not a use which offers a remedy for it. No larger system emerges in which suffering is the means to a higher good.

> I choose white, but with
> Red on it, like the snow
> In winter with its few
> Holly berries and the one
>
> Robin, that is a fire
> To warm by and like Christ
> Comes to us in his weakness,
> But with a sharp song.
> ('Song', p. 18)

The God of theodicies comes to us in his strength; in his sovereign omnipotence. That is why the sufferings in the world are thought to constitute such an embarrassment for faith in him. If God is said to be in such sufferings, everything depends, including one's conception of God, on how that involvement is understood. Here, God comes in weakness, not in strength. Yet, to accept the use he wishes to make of weakness will involve accepting 'a sharp song'. There are two poems in which these warring conceptions of God are to be seen within the same composition.

In the opening lines of the first of these the god depicted is one who inflicts evils on man for no other reason, apparently, than his dislike of him.

> He touched it. It exploded.
> Man was inside with his many
> Devices. He turned from him as from his own
> Excrement. He could not stomach his grin.
>
> I'll mark you, he thought. He put his finger
> On him.
> ('Repent')

In the middle section of the poem we are shown the diverse reactions to the suffering God has caused. The difficulty for the internal unity of the poem is to see how any reaction other than rebellion would make sense given the vindictive deity portrayed in the opening lines. This characterisation of God has to be forgotten in accepting the diversity of man's response to suffering.

> The result was poetry:
> The lament of Job, Aeschylus,
> The grovelling of the theologians.
> Man went limping through life, holding
> His side.

In the closing lines we are given a very different conception of God, not a God who explains away suffering, but one whose identity is bound up with it.

> But who were these in the laboratories
> Of the world? He followed the mazes
> Of their calculations, and returned
> To his centre to await their coming for him.

> It was not his first time to be crucified.[9]

Again, the difficulty is to see what the God whose centre has to do with crucifixion has to do with the god of the opening lines.

A similar tension is to be found in 'Echoes', which opens with the picture of a God bewildered by the lack of sense in the world. Its pain is caused by his blows of frustration.

> What is this? said God. The obstinacy
> Of its refusal to answer
> Enraged him. He struck it
> Those great blows it resounds
> With still. It glowered at
> Him, but remained dumb,
> Turning on its slow axis
> Of pain, reflecting the year
> In its seasons.
>   ('Echoes')

Here bewilderment in the Godhead is the only possible result of a request for justificatory explanations of pain. In response to such a request the world remains dumb, but the pain continues. At the end of the poem, however, when men come to worship God, we are told,

> On the altars
> They made him the red blood
> Told what he wished to hear.
>   (p. 14)

Here we are back with a 'sharp song', for if God is identified with suffering it must not be as a deity thirsty for the blood of others.

> Abel looked at the wound
> His brother had dealt him, and loved him
> For it. Cain saw that look
> And struck him again. The blood cried
> On the ground; God listened to it.
>   ('Cain')

But when Cain questions God as to why Abel's sacrifice was more acceptable than his sacrifice of vegetables and flowers, involving no blood, God's reply is one which identifies with suffering, but offers no remedy for it.

> And God said: It was part of myself
> He gave me. The lamb was torn
> From my own side. The limp head,
> The slow fall of red tears – they
> Were like a mirror to me in which I beheld
> My reflection. I anointed myself
> In readiness for the journey
> To the doomed tree you were at work upon.
>   (p. 22)

Slowly, but surely, R. S. Thomas asks us to reflect on a God very different from the omnipotent sovereign bestowed with power to do what he chooses. At the door of such a god we bring our myriad questions concerning what went wrong with his plans. And to silence us we are told that the plan is more complex than we thought. It is in this context that 'the grovellings of theologians' flourish, and, let it be said, there are plenty of contemporary philosophers of religion to keep them company. But the God the poet would have us see in the poems we are considering now, seems to be one whose nature is involved with these very features of human life which we want explained away. This is a God who can be crucified.

And God held in his hand
A small globe. Look, he said.
The son looked . . . .

On a bare
Hill a bare tree saddened
The sky. Many people
Held out their thin arms
To it, as though waiting
For a vanished April
To return to its crossed
Boughs. The son watched
Them. Let me go there, he said.
('The Coming', p. 36)

This coming of God is the emergence of a God very different in kind from the product of theodicies. This can be seen if we think of the traditional way in which philosophers have discussed the problem of evil. They have seen the problem as one which involves a belief in an omnipotent and loving God in insuper-able logical difficulties. These difficulties, given evil, come from wanting to say that God is both omnipotent *and* loving. Evil forces us to abandon one or other of these attributes. If God is all-powerful he must be able to do something about evil. If he is all-loving he must want to do something about evil. The unde-niable reality of evil, therefore, must mean either that God cannot do anything about it, in which case he is not omnipotent; or that he will not do anything about it, in which case he is not loving. These difficulties come from thinking of omnipotence and love as two *separate* attributes of God, the difficulty being to reconcile them in face of the evil which should be eradicated. Once these assumptions are accepted, one inherits the traditional problem of evil. But what R. S. Thomas is showing us is that we should not accept the assumption. God does not have two attributes, omnipotence and love. On the contrary, the God that R. S. Thomas's deepest poems reveal is a God whose only omnip-otence *is* that of love. That is why for those who want God (and sometime or other most people do) to be a power which will eradicate the sufferings men endure, the God R. S. Thomas shows us comes with a 'sharp song'.

To those who ask, 'Who did these things? Who is responsible

for them?' the answer 'God' is nearer to 'No one' than to 'Another person, far more powerful than ourselves.' Think of the term 'act of God' in law. It rules out tracing the event to a specific agent; it just happened, it was an act of God. If, on the other hand, we try to make God an agent among agents, we can ask for his reasons and justifications for why things are as they are. Such questions reflect a God, more powerful than ourselves, but man writ large nevertheless. R. S. Thomas says that such tendencies of thought miss the reflections of God. These reflections are not found in imaginary extra presences, but in embracing the absences our questions come up against. We come to God through a *via negativa*, by coming to see that the nature of his will is born not of an external system which gives a point to everything, but of a radical pointlessness in things. It is precisely because there is no reason why things should go as they do in life that there is a possibility of seeing all things as acts of grace, as things bestowed without reference to oneself as the reason for their occurrence. It is not by seeking explicit answers, but by seeing why such answers must be hidden, died to, that the possibility of belief in a God who is present in all things emerges.

> Why no! I never thought other than
> That God is that great absence
> In our lives, the empty silence
> Within, the place where we go
> Seeking, not in hope to
> Arrive or find. He keeps the interstices
> In our knowledge, the darkness
> Between stars. His are the echoes
> We follow, the footprints he has just
> Left. We put our hands in
> His side hoping to find
> It warm. We look at people
> And places as though he had looked
> At them, too; but miss the reflection.
>   ('Via Negativa', p. 23)

We miss the reflection if we think of God as someone in control of a game, possessing all the knowledge of the outcome and explanations of the slips we make. In R. S. Thomas we find a poet who not only dies to the conception of God as one presence

among others, no matter how much more powerful, but also, like
Simone Weil, sees creation not in terms of a powerful feat, but,
rather, in terms of a self-emptying love. A dying to the self is at
the heart of the Godhead for R. S. Thomas. God empties himself
of power in making room for man.

> I slept and dreamed
> Of a likeness, fashioning it,
> When I woke, to a slow
> Music; in love with it
> For itself, giving it freedom
> To love me; risking the disappointment.
> ('Making'[10])

Men who believe in a self-emptying God can only worship him
by sharing his nature. They, too, Simone Weil emphasises, must
empty themselves of a false divinity, before such communion is
possible. As long as we think of God as providing explanatory
answers for the world's ills, this religious insight will elude us.
We think of knowledge as power and control. God's knowledge is
then thought of as supreme power and control. The kind of
knowledge of God R. S. Thomas wants to show us in his poetry is
very different. This knowledge is only possible through a sac-
rifice, a dying to the self, so that God can come in at the right
place. The seeker of justifications of the ways of God to men
wants to know why things happened to him in just the ways they
did. The man who comes to see that no such reasons can be
found, who sees the givenness of his life as an act of grace, has
come to a knowledge of God. But there is much in us that rebels
against accepting such knowledge, and so the task of sacrificing
ourselves to God is a never-ending one. In so far as believers
achieve it, they testify to God's grace working in them. But,
often, it is the desire for the knowledge which is power that we
seek. In religion that desire will take the form of desire for a God
of power and control. The results are predictable:

> Friend, I had said,
> Life is too short for
> Religion; it takes time
> To prepare a sacrifice
> For the God. Give yourself

> To science that reveals
> All, asking no pay
> For it. Knowledge is power;
> The old oracle
> Has not changed. The nucleus
> In the atom awaits
> Our bidding. Come forth,
> We cry, and the dust spreads
> Its carpet. Over the creeds
> And masterpieces our wheels go.
>   ('No Answer', p. 17)

We are now in a position to take stock of the notion of religious patience which emerges in some of R. S. Thomas's poems, albeit a comparatively small number of them. We can approach it by seeing how it goes beyond certain vocational or even ethical conceptions of patience. The vocational conception of patience looms large in R. S. Thomas's poetry. We have met it again and again in his celebration of the peasant's endurance. What does such patience consist in? The Danish philosopher Søren Kierkegaard can help us to answer this question in his perceptive analysis of the difference between courage and patience. Kierkegaard raises the important question of whether a man can will suffering. He is speaking not of sufferings which we can do something about, but of those sufferings which, after our best endeavours are over, remain as undeniable facts. Put thus, the question seems paradoxical, if not self-contradictory. Kierkegaard brings out why we should think so: 'Is not suffering something that one must be forced into against his will? If a man can be free of it, can he then will it, and if he is bound to it, can he be said to will it? . . . Yes, for many men it is almost an impossibility for them to unite freedom and suffering in the same thought.'[11] The impossibility has to do with questions which Kierkegaard knows we are tempted to ask:

> Can anyone but one who is free of suffering, say, 'Put me in chains, I am not afraid'? Can even a prisoner say 'Of my own free will I accept my imprisonment' – the very imprisonment which is already his condition? Here again the opinion of most men is that such a thing is impossible, and that therefore the condition of the sufferer is one of sighing despondency.[12]

But if we feel that these conclusions must be accepted, Kierke-gaard has a question for us: 'But what then is patience?'[13] Kierkegaard provides an answer to his own question:

Is patience not precisely that courage which voluntarily ac-cepts unavoidable suffering? . . . Thus patience, if one may put it in this way, performs an even greater miracle than courage. Courage voluntarily chooses suffering that may be avoided; but patience achieves freedom in unavoidable suffering. By his courage, the free one voluntarily lets himself be caught, but by his patience the prisoner effects his freedom – although not in the sense that need make the jailer anxious or fearful.[14]

The patient figure in the fields whom R. S. Thomas has cele-brated certainly shows that he can win a war of endurance, where the meaning of the war is not given in its eventual out-come one way or another, but in the enduring of it. Of him, it might be said, with Kierkegaard,

The outward impossibility of ridding oneself of suffering does not hinder the inward possibility of being able really to emancipate oneself within suffering – of one's own free will accepting suffering, as the patient one gives his consent by willing to accept suffering. For one can be forced into a narrow prison, one can be forced into lifelong sufferings, and necessity is the tyrant; but one cannot be forced into patience. . . . And when the victim of unavoidable suffering bears it patiently, one says of him, 'to his shame, he is coerced, and he is making a virtue out of a necessity'. Undeniably he is making a virtue out of a necessity that is just the secret that is certainly a most accurate designation for what he does. He makes a virtue out of necessity. He brings a determination of freedom out of that which is determined as necessity.[15]

Is not the patient figure in the field to be preferred above those who think they can take eternity by storm; who seek instant answers which claim to be religious?

> Oh, I know it: the long story,
> The ecstasies, the mutilations;
> Crazed, pitiable creatures

> Imagining themselves a Napoleon,
> A Jesus; letting their hair grow,
> Shaving it off; gorging themselves
> On a dream; kindling
> A new truth, withering by it.
>
> While patiently this poor farmer
> Purged himself in his strong sweat,
> Ploughing under the tall boughs
> Of the tree of the knowledge of
> Good and evil, watching its fruit
> Ripen, abstaining from it.
>
> ('This One', p. 13)

Such a figure is going to be unintelligible to a world when the norm is to greet each rapid fashion

> The labour of the years
> Was over; the children were heirs
> To an instant existence.
>
> ('Digest', p. 19)

A parallel point can be made about ethical conceptions of patience. Here, the burden of what needs to be said lies in the possibility of the worth of decency transcending how the world happens to be treating one. There is, as Peter Winch points out, philosophical resistance to the ethical conception of patience:

> A way of expressing the paradoxical character of patience which would be more acceptable in terms of contemporary philosophical idiom, might be the following. When we reflect on the concepts on voluntary choice and inevitability, we feel inclined to say that they are mutually exclusive, that what is seen as inevitable cannot be voluntarily chosen. The concept of patience shows that this is not so. It would be a mere philosophical prejudice to argue in the opposite direction: that because inevitability excludes voluntary choice, patience is impossible. Patience clearly does exist. . . . And this *is* to bear the afflictions that life brings patiently – i.e. not to be deflected from acting decently even under the pressure of misfortune.[16]

Yet, neither endurance in misfortune nor refusal to be deflected from decency in such circumstances amount, in themselves, to a religious conception of patience. The main difference is in the sacrificial nature of religious patience. If we are to speak of sacrifice in the other two contexts, it would refer to a relation between something lost and something gained. Some things are sacrificed in enduring, and some things are sacrificed in clinging to decency. It does not follow from this, however, that the character of the enduring or the moral considerations has anything to do with sacrifice *in itself*. The religious notion of patience I am concerned with is sacrificial in character, sacrificial in itself. It is not something which survives misfortune, but grows out of an embracing of the misfortune itself.

When misfortune visits us, the natural cry is heard, 'Why is this happening to me?' Belief in God, for many, is supposed to give an answer to this question. Justifications of the ways of God are supposed to show why things have gone one way with you rather than another. Simone Weil, in her writings, shows how such justifications answer a deep need in us; the need for things to go one way rather than another. If something bad happens to us, we look forward, with some expectation of fulfilment, to some rectifying of the balance.[17] Again, religion of a certain kind plays a central role here for many people. When it is obvious that the balance is not to be rectified in this life, it offers a rectification of it in a future life. But as the Misfit in Flannery O'Connor's story 'A Good Man is Hard to Find'[18] complains, Jesus has thrown everything off balance by dying for no crime! Simone Weil emphasises that at the heart of what she calls 'supernatural religion' is the readiness to die to the expectation of a balance where every misfortune is to be compensated by good fortune. She says that everything offered to achieve this balance is a lie.– except grace. Grace comes in at the right place, however, if, instead of wanting an answer to the question, 'Why are things as they are?' we stop asking it. Simone Weil shows that in doing this we cease to think of providence as having to justify itself with respect to one's interests. What comes, comes from God as blessing or tribulation. Grace is the giveness of things under a religious aspect. Under a secular aspect it may be called luck. In the acceptance of things as the will of God, the self ceases to be the centre of the world. The self is sacrificed to God. In humans the sacrifice is seldom complete, since the powerful tendencies I have mentioned militate against it. If something has been ours long enough, we come to feel, as Simone Weil says, that it is ours by right. In our recent political experience it is not hard to see that a language of rights has dominated, if not often eliminated, a language of grace. It has been made harder for grace to come in at the right place. For example, acceptance of all things from God's hands may be thought, in these days of talk of activism, to involve a resigned quietism. This is not so, for seeing God and not the self at the centre involves combating the many styles, relationships and institutions where this truth is denied and where men are related to each other in different forms of self-appropriation and exploitation of others. Such endeavours, however, will not be totally successful. They may show little sign of getting anywhere. At such times, the kind of religious believer I am talking about will be sustained by the religious patience in the name of which he acts. He will realise that in all his strivings the outcome too is in God's hands.

There are similar conclusions to be found in Kierkegaard's writings. He points out that when people have said that with God all things are possible, they have either wanted God to do the impossible, or seen the possibility promised as the necessary, successful outcome of their various endeavours. Belief and property are married in the minds of some of R. S. Thomas's farmers. But Kierkegaard looks on the remark differently: namely, that in God, that is what all things become – possibilities. There are so many things we think are necessary, but in the kind of religious belief we are concerned with there is a readiness to wait on God, to see all things as mere possibilities. To see this is to see life as a gift; to see men as recipients of God's grace; to see life itself as a grace granted to man by God.

R. S. Thomas, it seems to me, approaches similar conclusions in the following remarks:

> But I firmly believe this, that eternity is not something out there, not something in the future; it is close to us, it is all around us and at any given moment one can pass into it; but there is something about our mortality, the fact that we are time-bound creatures, that makes it somehow difficult if not impossible to dwell, whilst we are in the flesh, to dwell permanently in that, in what I would call the Kingdom of Heaven.[19]

Compare these remarks with the following remarks by Kierke-gaard:

> And yet eternity is not like a new world, so that one who had lived in time according to the ways of time and of the press of busyness, if he were to make a happy landing in eternity itself, could now try his luck in adopting the customs and practices of eternity. Alas, the temporal order and the press of busyness believe, that eternity is so far away. And yet not even the foremost professional theatrical producer has ever had all in such readiness for the stage and for the change of scenes, as eternity has all in readiness for time: all – even to the least detail, even to the most insignificant word that is spoken; has all in readiness in each instant – although eternity delays.[20]

The Kingdom of Heaven is far off, eternity delays, because of everything which comes between man and God. But the hope offered, the use proposed for our hurt, is, it must be remembered, a love of the world in a mode of acceptance of all things from God; a love which puts itself and not man's worldly ambitions as the central concern. It is this 'sharp song' that R. S. Thomas celebrates in his profoundest poems.

> It's a long way off but inside it
> There are quite different things going on:
> Festivals at which the poor man
> Is king and the consumptive is
> Healed; mirrors in which the blind look
> At themselves and love looks at them
> Back; and industry is for mending
> The bent bones and the minds fractured
> By life. It's a long way off, but to get
> There takes no time and admission
> Is free, if you will purge yourself
> Of desire, and present yourself with
> Your need only and the simple offering
> Of your faith, green as a leaf.
>
> ('The Kingdom', p. 35)

This is no traditional 'solution' to the problem of evil. It places evil in a new context, one in which the dying to the self which

leads to God has to be mediated. Such mediation is not easy.
There are limiting cases which pose enormous question marks.
For example, what of those whose affliction is such that there is
no possibility of such *conscious* mediation in their own lives; no
question of their own awareness of religious meanings? R. S.
Thomas poses the issue starkly:

> and one said
> speak to us of love
> and the preacher opened
> his mouth and the word God
> fell out so they tried
> again speak to us
> of God then but the preacher
> was silent reaching
> his arms out but the little
> children the ones with
> big bellies and bow
> legs that were like
> a razor shell
> were too weak to come
>
> ('H'm', p. 34)

This is not the last time we shall meet the primitive gesture
which hopes to make contact with a religious reality.

I have said that by the end of the volume *The Stones of the Field*
R. S. Thomas presented a powerful challenge to certain forms of
the Christian religion. At that point there was little, if any,
indication of how that challenge was to be met. The question
whether to curse or bless haunts peasant, poet and priest. By
the end of the next volume, *An Acre of Land*, he feels that there
is a sense to be wrested from the peasant's way of life which
transcends his sense of endurance, but as yet he is not in a pos-
ition to express this sense. In the later poems included in *Song at the
Year's Turning*, however, two poems, 'Pisces' and 'In a Country
Church' offer the beginnings of a new vision. In *The Minister*
there is a reversion of emphasis to those forms of religion which
the poet thinks are 'wrong from the start'. In *Poetry for Supper*
the poem 'The Journey' continues the task of expressing his new
vision in verse. But in *Tares* and *The Bread of Truth* it is the
difficulties which beset such expression that predominate. In

Pietà, however, we again saw how the positive religious vision is extended in a number of poems: 'In Church', 'Ah!', 'Pietà' and 'The Moor'. But, again, struggles with faith reassert their hold and in *Not that he Brought Flowers*, the poet–priest writes in tension for a religious sense to emerge.

Without doubt, the deepest religious insights in the poetry of R. S. Thomas reach maturity in *H'm*. It is because he does not plot the course of this maturity that A. E. Dyson, despite his earlier recognition of the importance of the volume, concludes, wrongly, in my view, 'But maybe it is the new savagery which dominates *H'm*, which makes it Thomas's most memorable and terrible volume to date.'[21] I have tried to show the course of the maturing religious theme in R. S. Thomas's verse: first in the struggle with warring conceptions of God found in 'Repent' and 'Echoes', and then to a greater extent in the poems 'Song', 'Cain', 'The Coming', 'Via Negativa', 'Making', 'No Answer' and 'The Kingdom'. But as the poem 'H'm' shows, the new vision, although not open to the criticisms which can be levelled at the forms of religion the poet attacks, has struggles of its own to face. Struggle will always be part of faith, since the demands of faith's 'sharp song' are such that men will always wonder whether what they are giving themselves to is an illusion or not. Demands that go deep often involve such doubts. Commenting on the title of the collection, *H'm*, R. S. Thomas said, ' "You have to call a book something", then mimicked two ways of saying it – "H'm" as a sceptical question and "H'm" as a purr of contentment.'[22]

7   Presence and Absence

In 1976 R. S. Thomas delivered the annual literature lecture at
the National Eisteddfod at Cardigan. His title was *Abercuawg*. He
begins his lecture as follows: 'Where is Abercuawg? I'm not
certain that this is the right way of asking the question. I'm half
afraid that the answer to that is that it does not exist at all. And
as a Welshman I do not see any meaning in my life if there is no
such place as Abercuawg, a town or village where the cuckoos
sing.'[1] The poet tries to trace the origin of the name, but,
whenever a place is suggested to him, on his arrival there he
finds that it is not Abercuawg. We are fascinated with names
and, once given the name, we want to locate that to which the
name refers – in this case, apparently, a place. Yet, the role of
Abercuawg, the place where cuckoos sing, is not so straight-
forward as it seems. It is natural to assume that, if the first place we
have come across is not Abercuawg, and a second place is not
Abercuawg either, it makes sense to hope that some future place
we arrive at will, in fact, be Abercuawg. But this is precisely
what R. S. Thomas denies. Abercuawg is not a discoverable
locality in that sense. 'The fact that we travel to the locality of
Machynlleth to search for the location of Abercuawg and say:
"No, this is not it", means nothing. This is not an occasion for
disappointment and hopelessness, but a way of getting to know
better, through its absence, the nature of the place we are
looking for.'[2] Abercuawg cannot be located first, before we say
anything about the various geographical locations about us. On
the contrary, Abercuawg gets its meaning from the illumination
it casts on factual places. It is only by the emergence of a sense of
something lost or beyond what we actually know that Aber-
cuawg exercises a hold on us. Its presence, the difference it
makes to the world, can only be grasped in the form of absence.
R. S. Thomas says,

> This is man's condition. He is always about to comprehend
> God; but insomuch as he is a creature and finite, he will never

succeed. Nor will he ever see Abercuawg. But by trying to see it, by longing for it, by refusing to accept that it belongs to the past and has gone to oblivion, by refusing to accept something second-hand in its place, he will succeed in maintaining its eternal possibility.[3]

There is much in contemporary philosophy of religion which militates against what R. S. Thomas wants to show us. The assumption is made that we could settle the question of God's existence first, before proceeding to discuss what it makes sense to say to God and of God. It sounds so reasonable: what point is there in discussing worship of God if we cannot determine whether he exists? And so we have countless books in the philosophy of religion which begin by postulating an omnipotent and omniscient God and then proceed to argue whether we have or do not have any good reason for believing in the existence of such a being. But the existence of *what* being? That question has yet to be answered. The initial postulation has already assumed that we know what we are talking about. But do we, any more than we would know what Abercuawg is, if we failed to realise that its presence can only be known through its absence? If we fail to take account of how the notion of Abercuawg enters our lives, if it does enter them, then it is likely that we will assume that Abercuawg is simply a place alongside or in addition to other places. If that is how we think of it, it cannot be Abercuawg; that Abercuawg which is not another place, but that which shows the sense or lack of sense of any particular place. So with God. If we simply postulate a conception of God at the outset of a philosophical treatise, that notion is completely unmediated. We have not shown how it can get a hold on human life. It is all too easy to make God an extra object, greater, of course, than any finite object, but an additional one nevertheless. In that event, the notion of God, like that of Abercuawg, will not come in at the right place. As an extra object, the notion of God could not bring the kind of sense it does to so many human lives. Cut off from that sense it becomes the God of the philosophers, not the God of living faith. It is only by seeing how the notion of God has a certain application in the lives of some believers that we can come to some understanding of the sense it has. As we have seen, Simone Weil expresses the point in a striking way: 'Earthly things are the criterion of spiritual things. . . . Only spiritual things are of value, but only physical things have a verifiable existence. Therefore the value of the former can only be verified as an illumination projected on to the latter.'[4]

These problems which arise from concept formation in religion concern R. S. Thomas in his verse. They feature prominently in the volume *Laboratories of the Spirit*. The poet knows full well the kind of proof people mistakenly seek, of God's existence as much as that of Abercuawg.

> Something to bring back to show
> you have been there: a lock of God's
> hair, stolen from him while he was
> asleep; a photograph of the garden
> of the spirit.
>
> ('Somewhere')

This is not how a mediation of religious sense is to be achieved. We grasp that sense, if at all, only by taking note of its application in human life.

> Surely there exists somewhere,
> as the justification for our looking for it,
> the one light that can cast such shadows?'
>
> (p. 73[5])

This, as we have seen, is the poet's task: to show how those shadows are cast. The task, however, is not one which is unaffected by what is happening in other areas of life. He believes that the mediation he struggles for is particularly difficult now:

> I think of man
> on his mountain; he has paused
> now for lack of the oxygen
> of the spirit; the easier options
> surround him, the complacencies of being
> half-way up. He needs some breath
> from the summit, a stench rising
> to him from the valley from
> which he has toiled to release
> his potential; a memory rather

of those bright flags, that other
climbers of other mountains
have planted and gone
their way, not down but on
up the incline of their choosing.
('Relay', p. 54)

The breath from the summit cannot be taken for granted. On the
contrary, the mediation may take ambivalent or even savage
forms. Realising the interdependence of religious meanings and
the forms rejection of religion may take is no guarantee of
acceptance of the religious meanings involved. The reaction may
be to stress the price at which such meanings are obtained.

He had

to be killed; salvation acquired
by an increased guilt. The tree,
with its roots in the mind's dark,
was divinely planted, the original fork
in existence. There is no meaning in life,
unless men can be found to reject
love. God needs his martyrdom.
The mild eyes stare from the Cross
in perverse triumph. What does he care
that the people's offerings are so small?
('Amen', p. 52)

It may be said that the more powerful poems in *Laboratories of the
Spirit* are devoted to declarations of the difficulties involved in
making clear sense of what religion claims to offer. As always,
the poet refuses to indulge in any falsification of the facts:

A pen appeared, and the god said:
'Write what is to be
man.' And my hand hovered
long over the bare page,

until there, like footprints
of the lost traveller, letters
took shape on the page's
blankness, and I spelled out

> the word 'lonely'. And my hand moved
> to erase it; but the voices
> of all those waiting at life's
> window cried out loud: 'It is true.'
>
> ('The Word', p. 50)

The problem is that, if the facts are not to be falsified, many may
feel that they cannot be marshalled on the side of religion. Here
the poet is reverting to the issue of what religion becomes if its
character is to be inferred from the balance of good and evil in
human life. How could it be anything other than a mixed report?
The poet expresses this in telling of a struggle between God and
a hand which pleads with God to be given his name so that it
may be proclaimed unambiguously to mankind. But, given this
conception of religion, God himself, in the poet's view, cannot
see a clear vision in the mixed character of things. The hand has
to depart without God's blessing:

> It was a hand. God looked at it
> and looked away. There was a coldness
> about his heart, as though the hand
> clasped it. As at the end
> of a dark tunnel, he saw cities
> the hand would build, engines
> that it would raze them with. His sight
> dimmed. Tempted to undo the joints
> of the fingers, he picked it up.
> But the hand wrestled with him. 'Tell
> me your name,' it cried, 'and I will write it
> in bright gold. Are there not deeds
> to be done, children to make, poems
> to be written? The world
> is without meaning, awaiting
> my coming.' But God, feeling the nails
> in his side, the unnerving warmth
> of the contact, fought on in
> silence. This was the long war with himself
> always foreseen, the question not
> to be answered. What is the hand
> for? The immaculate conception
> preceding the delivery

of the first tool? 'I let you go,'
he said, 'but without blessing.
Messenger to the mixed things
of your making, tell them I am.'
                    ('The Hand', p. 49)

The poem indicates that God cannot do what the hand would
have it do; that the hand, in the nature of its request, misunder-
stands what God has to give. But the poem does not have the
explicit elucidation of an alternative such as we found in the
profoundest poems in *H'm*. There are moods, however, where
the alternative seems to be put aside, and full rein is given to the
implications of letting the facts of good and evil speak for
themselves. If we do have a picture of a supernatural designer
who has created the world as a kind of obstacle race for man,
then creation may seem to be malign. To try to make sense of
human affairs in terms of design may lead to a recognition of
such human senselessness that any conception of creation in-
volved will be one more appropriate to a malignant demon than
a moralistic god. In one of the most extreme of R. S. Thomas's
poems which reflect such moods, creation is depicted in terms of
malicious destruction and the coming of Jesus as a malformation
which provokes the uncontrollable laughter of God!

God looked at the eagle that looked at
the wolf that watched the jack-rabbit
cropping the grass, green and curling
as God's beard. He stepped back;
it was perfect, a self-regulating machine
of blood and faeces. One thing was missing:
he skimmed off a faint reflection of himself
in sea-water; breathed air into it,
and set the red corpuscles whirling. It was not long
before the creature had the eagle, the wolf and
the jack-rabbit squealing for mercy. Only the grass
resisted. It used it to warm its imagination
by. God took a handful of small germs,
sowing them in the smooth flesh. It was curious,
the harvest: the limbs modelled an obscene
question, the head swelled, out of the eyes came

tears of pus. There was the sound
of thunder, the loud, uncontrollable laughter of
God, and in his side like an incurred stitch, Jesus.

('Rough', p. 68)

The poet, as in *H'm*, oscillates between different reactions in which what the word 'God' means varies drastically. A. E. Dyson has said, ' "Rough" would seem to suggest a creation flawed not accidentally, but in its inception. It is not a random but a planned artefact, but the creator is schizoid, or at least an amoral perfectionist whose energies have run out of control.'[6] It is extremely important to note, as Dyson says, that 'Clearly, any single poem is not the last word: and, if it were, the others would be impoverished rather than enriched. But, equally clearly, a poem such as "Rough" could be the last word: no doubt some men might discover in it a lucid, sufficient statement of the universe, as they know it.'[7] When R. S. Thomas wants to show how a positive religious meaning is possible, he knows well that there are obstacles even from within some forms of religious perspective. He knows that people want something other than the spirituality he wants to celebrate: R. S. Thomas in writing a poem on St Mary's Well shows how the reflections people have and prefer, turn religion into superstition:

Ignoring my image, I peer down
to the quiet roots of it, where
the coins lie, the tarnished offerings
of the people to the pure spirit
that lives there, that has lived there
always, giving itself up
to the thirsty, witholding
itself from the superstition
of others, who ask for more.

('Ffynnon Fair' (St Mary's Well), p. 72)

If the believers throw enough coins into the Faith, that is the reflection which will return to them. In such contexts as these the priest will feel deserted. He, too, like the peasant who ploughs on and on for a bleak harvest, keeps going, saying the offices in his church, unwanted and unnoticed.

The priest would come
and pull on the hoarse bell nobody
heard, and enter that place
of darkness, sour with the mould
of the years. And the spider would run
from the chalice, and the wine lie
there for a time, cold and unwanted
by all but he, while the candles
guttered as the wind
picked at the roof.

('Poste Restante', p. 56)

There are times, however, when the priest's impatience turns into nastiness. Here is a test of vocation proposed by the poet:

Share their distraught
joy at the dropping of their inane
children. Test your belief

in spirit on their faces staring
at you, on beauty's surrender
to truth, on the soul's selling
of itself for a corner

by the body's fire. Learn the thinness
of the window that is
between you and life, and how
the mind cuts itself if it goes through

('The Calling'[8])

Why should the birth of children be described as a 'dropping', and why should the children be described as inane? In 'Petition' in *H'm*, we saw that the priest, seeing the affliction around him, seeks the poem in the pain, but concludes that silence is best, paying for it with his conscience. Here, however, the priest is not silent and his sentiments, rather than seeking the poem in the pain, have the regrettable effect of adding to the pain. In that respect it shares the spirit of 'The Country Clergy' in *Poetry for Supper*.

Yet, it would be quite wrong to say that these moods dominate the poet. Neither can their presence be denied. Moods of impatience and worse come with their threat. But other attitudes have their day too. With the increased apathy towards religion, the poet softens his attitude to the Nonconformity he attacked so vigorously in *The Minister*. The notion of salvation involved may have been narrow, but at least that can be transformed into something deeper. Mediocrity and apathy are far more difficult to change.

> A little aside from the main road,
> becalmed in a last-century greyness,
> there is the chapel, ugly, without the appeal
> to the tourist to stop his car
> and visit it . . . .
>
> But here once on an evening like this,
> in the darkness that was about
> his hearers, a preacher caught fire
> and burned steadily before them
> with a strange light, so that they saw
> the splendour of the barren mountains
> about them and sang their amens
> fiercely, narrow but saved
> in a way that men are not now.
>
> ('The Chapel', p. 59)

Also, the priest's despair at lack of response in his people may also be premature. Alone on his knees in his church the priest is tempted to conclude,

> Religion is over, and
> what will emerge from the body
> of the new moon, no one
> can say.

But the priest does not rest in this conclusion:

> But a voice sounds
> in my ear: Why so fast,
> mortal? These very seas

are baptized. The parish
has a saint's name time cannot
unfrock. In cities that
have outgrown their promise people
are becoming pilgrims
again, if not to this place,
then to the recreation of it
in their own spirits. You must remain
kneeling. Even as this moon
making its way through the earth's
cumbersome shadow, prayer, too,
has its phases.
   ('The Moon in Lleyn', pp. 66–7)

The priest must not give way to impatience, although there will
be moods and moments no doubt when he will be invaded by it.
Yet, he wants to do more than wait. He wants to go further and
celebrate an authentic religious sense in verse. Here we are back
with the problem of mediation, the struggle for a language which
can contain a rare religious directness. In my essay 'Seeking the
Poem in the Pain', I posed the question of whether R. S. Thomas
had achieved a satisfactory religious syntax in verse. I replied as
I have already noted,

> Does he find a poem in the pain, one which expresses relig-
> ion's answer to the woes of the world? Despite hints here and
> there the final answer must be, No. Perhaps the answer is
> negative . . . because, obsessed by the pain he sees around
> him, R. S. Thomas finds little which expresses joy. Praise
> seems foreign to his poetry, and on the rare occasions it
> appears there is a desperation about it which robs it of the
> purity it has sometimes had in the mouths of men.[9]

I wondered to what extent a satisfactory religious syntax is
possible in the English language today.

As I have said, I now believe these conclusions were mistaken.
The main reason for the mistake was that I had not waited on
those poems which I have already mentioned where the poet–
priest is able to speak directly of religious insights. That he is
able to do so with an almost complete freedom from falsification
is a rare poetic achievement in our time. In *Laboratories of the*

Spirit he adds to the poems in which this achievement is marked. Once again, the emphasis is on turning away from religion conceived as a mode of possession; an advancement of self-interest, however enlightened. Religion has to do with dying to the centrality of the self, such that God can come in at the right place. As Randal Jenkins has said, 'R. S. Thomas is fundamentally at odds with the modern world which has put man, human consciousness, in place of God at the centre of things.'[10] One way in which the poet shows this is in his seeing the natural world as a gift, as an act of grace bestowed on him.

> I asked for riches.
> You gave me the earth, the sea,
> > the immensity
> of the broad sky. I looked at them
> and learned I must withdraw
> > to possess them. I gave my eyes
> > and my ears, and dwelt
> in a soundless darkness
> > in the shadow
> of your regard.
> > The soul
> grew in me, filling me
> with its fragrance.
> > Man came
> to me from the four
> > winds to hear me speak
> > of the unseen flower by which
> I sat, whose roots were not
> in the soil, nor its petals the colour
> of the wide sea; that was
> > its own species with its own
> > sky over it, shot
> with the rainbow of your coming and going.
> > ('The Flower', p. 63)

But becoming poor in spirit is also to learn, if necessary, that suffering too may be one's lot. This is expressed powerfully in a poem full of tensions. There is a hint of a priest's impatience at the fragmentary and perhaps sentimental nature of the peasant's involvement in worship at Christmas and yet that taking of the

sacrament speaks to the daily life in which the peasant's body is
taxed by the inclement weather of the hills. The celebration in
the poem cannot be denied, and yet there is also a question, a
latent querying of the price of such a sacrifice.

> They came over the snow to the bread's
> purer snow, fumbled it in their huge
> hands, put their lips to it
> like beasts, stared into the dark chalice
> where the wine shone, felt it sharp
> on their tongue, shivered as at a sin
> remembered, and heard love cry
> momentarily in their heart's manger.
>
> They rose and went back to their poor
> holdings, naked in the bleak light
> of December. Their horizon contracted
> to the one small, stone-riddled field
> with its tree, where the weather was nailing
> the appalled body that had not asked to be born.
> ('Hill Christmas', p. 70)

As we saw in the last chapter, Kierkegaard shows us how
religious patience affects freedom even in prison. R. S. Thomas
presents us with the same truth.

> 'Poems from prison! About
> what?'
>   'Life and God.' 'God
> in prison? Friend, you trifle
> with me. His face, perhaps,
> at the bars, fading
> like life.'
>   'He came in
> with the warder, striving
> with him. Where else
> did the severity of the man
> spring from, but awareness
> of a charity he must
> overcome?'

'The blows, then,
were God chastening
the beloved! Who
was the more blessed, the
dispenser or receiver
of them?'
                    'It is the same
outside. Bars, walls
but make the perspective
clear. *Deus absconditus*!
We ransack the heavens,
the distance between
stars; the last place we look
is in prison, his hideout
in flesh and bone.'
                              'You believe,
then?'
                    'The poems
are witness. If his world
contracted, it was to give birth
to the larger vision. Not meadows
empty of him, animal
eyes, impersonal
as glass, communicate
God. On the bare walls
of a cell the oppressor watches
the diminishing of his
human shadow, as
he withdraws from the light.'
                    ('The Prisoner', pp. 77–8)

In this poem, the bland philosophy of nature whereby it commu-
nicates a meaning automatically to anyone in its vicinity is
rejected. Possession is again by withdrawal of the self. Wonder
and awe come in at the right place not by the balancing of
fortunes and misfortunes, but by an acceptance of the whole in
which, again, the self withdraws, and all things are seen as a gift,
as expressions of the omnipotent will of God. This is what
Simone Weil means by love of the beauty of the world. This form
of love is nonsense in terms of possession brought about by
self-assertion. It is inseparable from poverty of spirit. The poet

mediates the spirit of Christ through the poorest figure in the field:

> and there the scarecrow walked
> over the surface of the brown
> breakers tattered like Christ
> himself and the man went
> at his call with the fathoms
> under him and because
> of his faith in the creation
> of his own hands he was
> buoyed up floundering
> but never sinking scalded
> by the urine of the skies deaf
> to the voices calling from
> the high road telling him
> his Saviour's face was of straw.
>   ('Farming Peter', p. 64)

Because such poverty of spirit involves acceptance of all things, a simple incident may be an occasion for the revelation that all things are from God. A sudden breakthrough of the sun to illuminate a small field is one such instance for the poet.

> It is the turning
> aside like Moses to the miracle
> of the lit bush, to a brightness
> that seemed as transitory as your youth
> once, but is the eternity that awaits you.
>   ('The Bright Field', p. 81)

Even an empty church need not come between the priest and God, since the emptiness itself can mediate, without any other intermediary, the relation of the soul to God:

> I keep my eyes
> open and am not dazzled
> so delicately does the light enter
> my soul from the serene presence
> that waits for me till I come next.
>   ('Llananno', p. 83)

The sheer givenness of things speaks of an absence to the poet.
By seeing grace in all things, the giver of grace cannot be seen as
a thing alongside those that are given. Such an experience of
presence mediated through absence, God making all the differ-
ence to the world because he cannot be in it alongside all other
things, comes to the poet as he watches the sea.

> There were days,
> so beautiful the emptiness
> it might have filled,
>   its absence
> was as its presence; not to be told
> any more, so single my mind
> after its long fast,
>   my watching from praying.
>   ('Sea-Watching', p. 85)

In his Introduction to the *Selected Poems of Edward Thomas*, R. S.
Thomas says, 'Somewhere beyond the borders of Thomas' mind,
there was a world he never could quite come at. Many of his best
poems are a faithful recording of his attempts to do so.'[11] In my
essay 'Seeking the Poem in the Pain' I stated, 'It must be said
that that world has receded further in the poetry of R. S.
Thomas.'[12] That judgement cannot be allowed to stand, any
more than my judgement that the language of the poem 'Alive' is
simply 'pendantic, a tired language which no longer speaks.'[13]
This judgement was made by isolating the poem from those
which mediate the sense, for the poet, of all things coming from
God's hand. Placed in this context the poem speaks of the praise
which emanates from seeing God in all things. It is R. S. Thomas
who has shown how the longed-for good place, the abode of God,
can be made present via its absence.

> It is alive. It is you,
> God. Looking out I can see
> no death. The earth moves, the
> sea moves, the wind goes
> on its exuberant
> journeys. Many creatures
> reflect you, the flowers
> your colour, the tides the precision

of your calculations. There
is nothing too ample
for you to overflow, nothing
so small that your workmanship
is not revealed. I listen
and it is you speaking.
I find the place where you lay
warm. At night, if I waken,
there are the sleepless conurbations
of the stars. The darkness
is the deepening shadow
of your presence; the silence a
process in the metabolism
of the being of love.

                ('Alive', p. 76)

As in the previous volume, *H'm*, the poet is also aware of the
difficulties and the tensions created in saying that God can be
seen in all things. Some of these are occasioned by the difference
between an individual coming to this revelation for himself, and
the difficulty of being able to say that God is in the affliction of
others. If seeing God in all things is a song given to the believer,
how are the afflictions of others to appear in his song? The poet is
unsure whether he has a right to refer to the afflictions of others
who are denied the possibility of the song he would sing.

Was she planned?
Or is this one of life's
throw-offs? Small, taken from school
young; put to minister
to a widowed mother, who keeps
her simple, she feeds the hens,
speaks their language, is one
of them, quick, easily
frightened, with sharp
eyes, ears. When I have
been there, she keeps her perch
on my mind. I would
stroke her feathers, quieten
her, say: 'Life is
like this.' But have I

the right, who have seen plainer
women with love
in abundance, with
freedom, with money to
hand? If there is one thing
she has, it is a bird's
nature, volatile
as a bird. But even
as those among whom she
lives and moves, who look at her
with their expectant
glances, song is denied her.
('Marged', p. 74)

As in *H'm*, there is a tension at the heart of *Laboratories of the Spirit*. In both volumes we have poems which express deep religious insights, alongside those which are savage in their rejection of a religion where the god is a god of power who arranges that all is to turn out well in the end for those who have run the human obstacle race he has devised. Not only do these conceptions of God war with one another for man's allegiance; there are also difficulties within the conception which the poet celebrates as the deeper one. The difficulty is this: on one conception of God, the history of human beings cannot be a mixed one; all their misfortunes must somehow be means to a higher good; they must be explained away in some way or another. R. S. Thomas, quite rightly, refuses to believe this. If that is to be the requirement, then, as we saw in 'The Hand', God rejects the request for an unambiguous answer. The sense of the will of God which opposes this tradition, so far from being in conflict with the mixed character of human life, its features and misfortunes, grows out of a mode of acceptance of this radical variety and contingency. It is because he misses this possibility that A. E. Dyson thinks that

In *Laboratories of the Spirit* certain themes, perceptible earlier, emerge far more clearly – the limitations of language; the positive absence (or perversity) of God; flaws or apparent flaws in the very nature of a creation, and salvation; the indissoluble union of God and Jesus, in a manner unknown to previous theology. This faith – if such it is – is not in any normal sense incarnational.[14]

Such a conclusion depends on ignoring the centrality of the notion of a hidden God in R. S. Thomas's poetry. 'Creation' and 'salvation' in R. S. Thomas's poetry will inevitably seem flawed, as they do to Dyson, if that notion is ignored. It is hard to know what Dyson means by the 'normal sense' of 'incarnational', but any suggestion that R. S. Thomas wishes to etherealise faith is the opposite of the truth. As we have seen, and will see again, his whole concern is to do with how faith is to speak to the ordinary physical facts of human life. Yet, having noted R. S. Thomas's reaction to contingencies, and the conception of God involved in it, features of that world of contingencies, such as the fate of the retarded Marged, threaten that conception of God's will. And so the struggle for an adequate religious syntax continues in *Laboratories of the Spirit* as it has done previously in R. S. Thomas's work.

The same tensions are to be found in *The Way of It* (1977). On the one hand, the poet wants to say of God,

> You speak
> all languages and none,
> answering our most complex
> prayers with the simplicity
> of a flower, confronting
> us, when we would domesticate you
> to our uses, with the rioting
> viruses under our lens.
>
> ('Praise'[15])

If we are tempted to say that we have difficult questions which God does not seem to answer, the poet responds,

> We call him the dumb
> God with an effrontery beyond
> pardon. Whose silence so eloquent
> as his? What word so explosive
> as that one Palestinian
> word with the endlessness of its fall-out?
>
> ('Nuclear'[16])

On the other hand, how is the hurt we cause another person to be excused? One may be patient with the pain one has suffered oneself, a pain one shares with the animals. But what of the human hurt one has caused others?

> It is the memories
> that one has, the impenitent bungler
> of love, refusing for too long
> to say 'yes' to that earlier gesture
> of love that had brought one
> forth; it is these, as they grow
> clearer with the telescoping
> of the years, that constitute
> for the beholder the true human pain.
>
> ('Resolution'[17])

And so the struggle to mediate a satisfactory religious language goes on. In *Laboratories of the Spirit* there is a poem which shows us exactly what is at stake:

> You have no name.
> We have wrestled with you all
> day, and now night approaches,
> the darkness from which we emerged
> seeking; and anonymous
> you withdraw, leaving us nursing
> our bruises, our dislocations.
>
> For the failure of language
> there is no redress. The physicists
> tell us your size, the chemists
> the ingredients of your
> thinking. But who you are
> does not appear, nor why
> on the innocent marches
> of vocabulary you should choose
> to engage us, belabouring us
> with your silence. We die, we die
> with the knowledge that your resistance
> is endless at the frontier of the great poem.
>
> ('The Combat', p. 71)

In the further volumes we are to look at, our central question will be to plot the twists and turns of this combat. Despite the fact that, at times, a religious expression of great directness breaks through, there is enough pulling in an opposite direction to make the next stage of R. S. Thomas's poetic pilgrimage a genuinely open one.

8 God's Dialectic

In the Introduction to this essay, I mentioned the centrality of the notion of a hidden God, a *Deus absconditus*, in the poetry of R. S. Thomas. The idea is a difficult one and there are many pitfalls to be avoided in dealing with it. There are also different contexts in which talk of a hidden God varies a great deal in its significance. The volume *Frequencies* (1978) concentrates on these questions in a way which develops further the questions we have been discussing.

As we have seen, one way in which the notion of a hidden God has entered philosophy is to meet the objections of those who ask for a verification of God's existence. Philosophers in an attempt to defend the intelligibility of the notion of God said that such requests for direct verification are misleading since we have no direct knowledge of God. God is known only through his works. We can know God only indirectly while we are on earth. As we have already seen, forceful replies have been made to such apologetic manoeuvres. It has been said that in order to believe in God on the basis of what we see around us is indeed to believe in the miracle of a hidden God. David Hume, who held this view, advanced it with an irony which some have mistakenly thought to be a readiness to leave room for mystery and miracle. Hume is clearly using such terms pejoratively. He is saying that it would indeed take a miracle to believe in theism; believe that and you would believe anything! Hume is saying that religious belief is indeed a mystery; it is a wonder how anyone could ever come to embrace such things.

Some of the most powerful reasons for these conclusions, however, are, as we have seen, not unknown to religious believers. When many of them have looked without prejudice at the mixed character of human life, they have felt the facts to be a screen which hides God from them. Some have gone further and said that the sense in which the facts hide God is that they hide the meaning of 'God' from them. When this conviction reaches a certain stage, people lose their faith in God. Brute realities have hidden the very possibility of giving sense to belief in God.

There are times, as we have seen, when R. S. Thomas is able to enter into these moods. He would like to be able to put these questions aside:

> I engage with philosophy
> in the morning, with the garden
> in the afternoon. Evenings I
> fish or coming home empty-handed
> put on the music of
> César Franck. It is enough,
> this. I would be the mirror
> of a mirror, effortlessly repeating
> my reflections . . . .
>
> ('Present')

But other questions persist in engaging him. He has no choice but to pay heed to them:

> But there is that
> one who will not leave me
> alone, writing to me
> of her fear; and the news from the city
> is not good. I am at the switchboard
> of the exchanges of the people
> of all time, receiving their messages
> whether I will or no . . . .

And when these messages come, requests for a pattern to be imposed on the mixed phenomena such that good can somehow compensate for the evil, or for the pattern to show goodness as being in greater abundance, the poet knows he cannot give the answer the senders want to hear.

> Do you
> love me? the voices cry.
> And there is no answer; there are
> only the treaties and take-overs,
> and the vision of clasped
> hands over the unquiet blood.
>
> (p. 97[1])

But the seeking for answers is not without price. In reflecting on men fishing, the poet thinks that we too, when we think we have caught something, have nothing. It can even be doubted whether what we do catch is anything that will serve as an answer, since we seem to 'wait for the witheld answer to an insoluble problem'.

> But we fish on, and gradually
> they accumulate, the bodies, in the torn
> light that is about us and the air
> echoes to their inaudible screaming.
>   ('Fishing'[2])

The answers we do provide are at enormous cost: an ignoring of the sufferings around us. I must say that I share this reaction when I see the comforting rationalisations philosophers of religion offer in face of human suffering. They, too, seem to fish on oblivious of the accumulating bodies. And when the poet thinks of the long centuries that have gone by, the cost of the pain that has been caused and the possibility of extinction which looms ahead, the challenge to faith is formidable:

> What I need
> now is a faith to enable me to out-stare
> the grinning faces of the inmates of its asylum,
> the failed experiments God put away.
>   ('Pre-Cambrian', p. 106)

Little wonder that such questions place the would-be believer in an impossible position. He is torn apart, neither able to let his desire for God go, nor also to close his ears to questions which threaten to hide the very possibility of God from him. R. S. Thomas is doing more than calling our attention to the plight of a particular worshipper. He is asking us to consider whether, given this conception of the dialectic from which a belief in God is to emerge, there can be any other conclusion than an inconclusive verdict.

> Be it sufficient
> that in a church porch on an evening
> in winter, the moon rising, the frost

sharp, he was driven
to his knees and for no reason
he knew. The cold came at him;
his breath was carved angularly
as the tombstones; an owl screamed.

He had no power to pray.
His back turned on the interior
he looked out on a universe
that was without knowledge
of him and kept his place
there for an hour on that lean
threshold, neither outside nor in.

('The Porch', p. 98)

The universe cannot yield the knowledge needed if God's exist-
ence is to be verified. But must not our backs be turned on the
interior of faith if the grounds for it cannot be inferred from the
external world? In an effort to meet this objection an appeal may
be made to mystery. Why should we expect to base belief in God
on knowledge? Does not the very word 'faith' mean that such
knowledge is unattainable? Faith asks us to believe in a hidden
God. Some philosophers have argued that the nature of philo-
sophical theism depends on the view that finite man can never
hope to understand an infinite God. They infer from this re-
ligious truth the philosophical conclusion that human language is
inherently inadequate to capture the nature of an infinite God. It
is easy to see how this view postpones the questions of the critics.
The knowledge which, according to critics, is needed as a basis
for belief in God is available, but not available here. The
verification of God's existence will be provided eschatologically.
Meantime, we must have faith, believing that proof awaits us
later. On this view, language is a screen which hides us from
God. Here is a second sense of the notion of a hidden God. In the
first, we saw that the mixed character of man's fate hides, in the
sense of 'clouds', or even 'makes impossible', the idea of God.
In the second, God is hidden only in the contingent sense that,
given our position, we cannot comprehend him. There are signs
that *this* philosophical conception of a *Deus absconditus* influences
R. S. Thomas from time to time. He compares 'God' as ex-
pressed in our definitions with a tamed tiger. The tiger has

                    a body too huge
        and majestic for the cage in which
        it had been put;
                    ('The White Tiger')

and one can think of it

                    breathing

        as you can imagine that
        God breathes within the confines
        of our definitions of him, agonising
        over immensities that will not return.
                    (p. 120)

Is God caged by language? There is no doubt that God could be
caged by language. This happens when a given conception of
God is woefully inadequate. There is a suggestion of this in
Thomas's closing lines, where God is depicted as agonising over
immensities that will not return. Here, there is a reference to a
time when the immensities *were* present, so there is no suggestion
of the necessary inadequacy of language. What the poem calls
attention to is the possibility of an inadequate language con-
cerning God. Yet, there are times when the poet wants to go
further, and to say that God is beyond any concept we possess.
The difficulty, then, of course, is to give an account of how we
come to believe in or speak of God in the first place. The tension
shows in his desire to say, on the one hand, of talk of God,

                    It is its own
        light, a statement beyond language
        of conceptual truth.
                    ('Night Sky')

and, on the other hand, his desire to say,

                    I pick up the signals
        relayed to me from a periphery I comprehend.
                    (p. 103)

But how are the signals to be picked up? – that is the problem
given this conception of divine mystery. Are we to speak of a

radical inadequacy of the mind as Kierkegaard did? The poet
seems to think so:

> No pirácy, but there is a plank
> to walk over seventy thousand fathoms,
> as Kierkegaard would say, and far out
> from the land. I have abandoned
> my theories, the easier certainties
> of belief.
>
> ('Balance')

But, then, the inevitable question follows:

> Is there a place
> here for the spirit? Is there time
> on this brief platform for anything
> other than mind's failure to explain
> itself?[3]

As we have seen in *H'm*, R. S. Thomas wants to explore the sense
in which God makes a difference to the world by virtue of his
absence from it. He still does:

> It is this great absence
> that is like a presence, that compels
> me to address it without hope
> of a reply.
>
> ('The Absence')

For these lines to be successful, however, the 'reply' must be
conceived as a misunderstanding if it is sought for. In other
words, if one understands God's presence as a *Deus absconditus*,
replies of the kind the poet has in mind will not be expected
anyway. Later in the poem, however, this sense of absence is
elucidated in terms of the inadequacy of language.

> I modernise the anachronism
>
> of my language, but he is no more here
> than before. Genes and molecules
> have no more power to call
> him up than the incense of the Hebrews

at their altars. My equations fail
as my words do. What resource have I
other than the emptiness without him of my whole
being, a vacuum he may not abhor?

(p. 123)

But is not talk of God filling a vacuum talk of God in language?
Compare the following question: if someone says that words
cannot express how grateful he is, has he failed to express his
thanks in language? Obviously not. His expression is not a
failure, but one form of expressing thanks. This can be shown
from the fact that we know when it would be inappropriate to
use this expression of thanks. Similarly, I suggest, to say that
God makes a difference to the world by virtue of his absence from
it, is not to fail to talk of the reality of God, but to show how talk
of such a reality gets a hold on human life. When Job seeks a
God 'who doeth great things and unsearchable' (5:9); when the
Psalmist testifies, 'Great is the Lord; and greatly to be praised:
and his greatness is unsearchable' (145:3); when Paul exclaims,
'how unsearchable are his judgements and his ways past finding
out' – they are not *failing* to glorify God because of the inadequa-
cy of language. Theirs are expressions of praise *in* the language.
They are showing us how a hidden God is to be praised. As
Simone Weil says, 'the very reason why God has decided to hide
himself is that we might have an idea of what he is like'.[4] What is
fatal is to mix two ways of talking of God; to try to turn the *Deus
absconditus* into an additional presence alongside other beings.

> Sound, too? The recorder
> that picks up everything picked
> up nothing but the natural
> background. What language
> does the god speak?
> > ('The Film of God')

Having posed the question, the poet provides an answer:

> It was blank, then,
> the screen, as far as he
> was concerned? It was a bare
> landscape and harsh, and geological

its time. But the rock was
bright, the illuminated manuscript
of the lichen. And a shadow,
as we watched, fell, as though
of an unseen writer bending over
his work.

But, now, what happens if one asks what the shadow is a shadow of, as if 'God' were the name of something which could, in principle, be perceived directly?

And we waited
for it to move, silently
as the spool turned, waited
for the figure that cast it
to come into view for us to
identify it, and it
didn't and we are still waiting.
(p. 122)

The confusion here is in the continued waiting, since God had already been identified in talk of the shadow. The confusion comes from the surface grammar of 'There is a God.' It looks like a statement in the indicative mood, but in fact is not. R. S. Thomas seems to realise this at times and expresses it by speaking of the gap between the name and the thing signified. Philosophically, it would be better to point out that the word 'God' is not a name at all. Once we see this, we stop thinking of an object, the 'thing in itself', to which the name refers.

God woke, but the nightmare
did not recede. Word by word
the tower of speech grew.
He looked at it from the air
he reclined on. One word more and
it would be on a level
with him; vocabulary
would have triumphed . . . .
('The Gap')

But *what* would have triumphed? Only, as the poet says, 'the verbal hunger for the thing in itself'. But God leaves a blank beside his name to remain 'the grammarian's torment'. Yet, only a torment if one looks for a thing as the referent for the word 'God'. The poet still wants to insist

> that we stare
> over into the eternal
> silence that is the repose of God.
> (p. 96)

The question of the grammatical (in the sense of logical) status of that language confronts philosopher and poet alike. The poet is certainly aware of the fact. Failure to give full weight to this awareness leads Moelwyn Merchant into a rather conceptually inconclusive discussion of the issues involved. He says, 'The topic explored is nothing less than "The Gap" between God and our articulations of his being.'[5] It is essential to realise that this gap is not inevitable. In his most mature religious poems R. S. Thomas realises only too well what kind of language concerning God will not do. God is not to be regarded as an additional fact alongside other facts. But what is to be the alternative? The poet is involved with a struggle in verse to answer that question.

> There is an aggression of fact
> to be resisted successfully
> only in verse, that fights language
> with its own tools. Smile, poet,
>
> among the ruins of a vocabulary
> you blew your trumpet against.
> It was a conscript army; your words,
> every one of them, are volunteers.
> ('After Jericho', p. 118)

The main poems in *Frequencies* are poems 'after Jericho', a presenting of the alternatives which emerge when logical mistakes about the status of religious language have been exposed. But these poems themselves fall into two categories: first, those in which the temptation still exists to think of 'God' as a proper name requiring a referent, and second, poems which go beyond this stipulation to show how talk of God enters worship and thus our language in very different ways.

The poet sees clearly the kind of talk of God which will not do:

Face to face? Ah, no
God; such language falsifies
the relation. Nor side by side,
nor near you, nor anywhere
in time and space.

('Waiting')

And yet the farmers, during their daily rounds, spoke of God:

The
earth bore and they reaped:
God, they said, looking
in your direction. The wind
changed; over the drowned
body it was you
they spat at.

Perhaps the poet does not find this God of fits and starts
acceptable, but he has to wait for an acceptable language to
emerge for him.

Young
I pronounced you. Older
I still do, but seldomer
now, leaning far out
over an immense depth, letting
your name go and waiting,
somewhere between faith and doubt,
for the echoes of its arrival.

(p. 111)

But the nature of the echo will be determined by the character of
the word uttered in the first place. Sometimes the word is so
ambivalent that the waiting shares its character.

They laid this stone trap
for him, enticing him with candles,
as though he would come like some huge moth
out of the darkness to beat there.
Ah, he had burned himself
before in the human flame

and escaped, leaving the reason
torn. He will not come any more

to our lure. Why, then, do I kneel still
striking my prayers on a stone
heart? Is it in hope one
of them will ignite yet and throw
on its illumined walls the shadow
of someone greater than I can understand?
                          ('The Empty Church', p. 113)

But what if someone found God? What would that be like? Philosophers have asked whether, if a seer were to see some figure, however wonderful, that would be to see God. The poet wants to give up such searches although he realises that many go on in the name of religion.

He is a religious man.
How often I have heard him say,
looking around him with his worried eyes
at the emptiness: There must be something.

It is the same at night, when,
rising from his fused prayers,
he faces the illuminated city
above him: All that brightness, he thinks,

and nobody there! I am nothing
religious. All I have is a piece
of the universal mind that reflects
infinite darkness between points of light.
                          ('The Possession', p. 112)

Similarly, in religion, there is a confusion when one thinks of God as an agent among agents, and asks him for a justification of the various moves he makes in the game he is said to play. But the trouble is in the nature of the conceptual assumptions being made about God.

Your move I would have
said, but he was not

playing; my game a dilemma
that was without horns.

As though one can sit at table
with God!

('Play'[6])

Progress is made only when we put aside these misleading
assumptions. But this is only the beginning. The assumptions
will reappear in new forms:

They
yield, but only to re-form
as new problems; and one
does not even do that
but towers immovable
before us.

('The Answer')

We must learn to work through the wrong questions, not in
order to answer them, but in order to put them aside.

There have been times
when, after long on my knees
in a cold chancel, a stone has rolled
from my mind, and I have looked
in and seen the old questions lie
folded and in a place
by themselves, like the piled
graveclothes of love's risen body.

(p. 121)

If knowing God were a matter of intellectual assent, it ought to
be possible to say, 'I believe in God', without this having any
effect whatever on one's life. But this would not correspond to
anything akin to religious belief. The word 'feeling' has been
given such trite treatment in twentieth-century philosophy that
mention of it is almost bound to mislead. Yet the poet is right in
insisting that what needs to be made central are the affective
contexts in which the need for God has its sense, and a man

coming to God has its significance. Trying to argue for the existence of God by means of something like the argument from design seems fruitless. It does not seem to bring one any nearer to God:

> the higher
> one ascends, the poorer the visibility
> becomes.
>
> ('Perhaps')

One needs to look in a different direction:

> To learn to distrust the distrust
> of feeling – this then was the next step
> for the seeker?
>
> (p. 115)

Again, thinking that God's nature can be inferred from the way things go, seems to lead to absurd conclusions. It is difficult to make any sense of the game. As far as God is concerned,

> It is the play of a being
> who is not serious in
> his conclusions.
> ('The Game', p. 110)

It is these conclusions we want to change, and we call on God to change them. We want him to do something about rectifying the evil in the world:

> Let the deaf men
> be helped; in the silence that has come
> upon them, let some influence
> work so those closed porches
> be opened once more. Let the bomb
> swerve. Let the raised knife of the murderer
> be somehow deflected.
>
> ('Adjustments')

But such things are achieved in other ways:

        we must ask rather
for the transformation of the will
to evil, for more loving
mutations, for the better ventilating
of the atmosphere of the closed mind.
                            (pp. 108–9)

It is only by seeing that coming to God involves a transformation of the will that we are gradually eased away from those misleading attempts to frame a god in our own image. It is fitting that the mind should be 'sceptical as always of the anthropomorphisms of the fancy'. But a new realisation dawns. We see that trying to reach God is not an attempt to by-pass material things so that pure spirit may be approached directly – the Manichean heresy – but an attempt to see religious sense mediated in the ordinary things of life. It has been pointed out that R. S. Thomas is now presenting in verse one of the primary characteristics of this new period, 'the realization that man is not always ever against God, battering at him from outside'.[7]

        We are beginning to see
now it is matter is the scaffolding
of spirit; that the poem emerges
from morphemes and phonemes; that
as form in sculpture is the prisoner
of the hard rock, so in everyday life
it is the plain facts and natural happenings
that conceal God and reveal him to us
little by little under the mind's tooling.
                    ('Emerging', p. 117)

R. S. Thomas, as we have seen, believes that eternity is all around us; it is not a somewhere else, a region of the fancy.

            Did I confuse the categories?
            Was I blind?
            Was I afraid of hubris
            in identifying this land
            with the kingdom? . . .

I grow old,
bending to enter the promised
land that was here all the time
('The Small Country', p. 104)

As we have seen, this does not mean that R. S. Thomas identifies
religion with prevailing states of affairs. He sees how changes in
the countryside may make it more difficult for people to think
of God. We have an echo of his old relationship with Iago
Prytherch:

> Will they say on some future
> occasion, looking over the flogged acres
> of ploughland: This was Prytherch country?
> Nothing to show for it now: hedges
> uprooted, walls gone, a mobile people
> hurrying to and fro on their fast
> tractors; a forest of aerials
> as though an invading fleet invisibly
> had come to anchor among these
> financed hills. They copy the image
> of themselves projected on their smooth
> screens to the accompaniment of inane
> music. They give grins and smiles
> back in return for the money that is
> spent on them. But where is the face
> with the crazed eyes that through the unseen
> drizzle of its tears looked out
> on this land and found no beauty
> in it, but accepted it, as a man
> will who has needs in him that only
> bare ground, black thorns and the sky's
> emptiness can fulfil?
>
> ('Gone?'[8])

R. S. Thomas is not wishing Iago Prytherch's lot on him, but he
is saying that it had in it the possibility of asking for a meaning
for the whole of life which is on a different plane from the
balancing of advantage and disadvantage. It is a question about
the world at a level which contains these advantages and disad-
vantages. To see these as without reason, without an anthropo-

morphic point, is to see them as having a meaning which is
absent from the context of explanation and justification. Such
insight, as we have seen, is a precondition of letting wonder and
grace come in at the right place, a precondition of seeing how it
is possible to see all things as coming from God. In celebrating
Abercuawg in verse the poet says,

> An absence is how we become surer
> of what we want. Abercuawg
> is not here now, but there. And
> there is the indefinable point,
> the incarnation of a concept,
> the moment at which a little
> becomes a lot . . . .
>
>   I have no faith
> that to put a name to
> a thing is to bring it
> before one. I am a seeker
> in time for that which is
> beyond time, that is everywhere
> and nowhere; no more before
> than after, yet always
> about to be; whose duration is
> of the mind, but free as
> Bergson would say of the mind's
> degradation of the eternal.
>   ('Abercuawg'[9])

What we have seen is that in the poet's religiously mature
poems, language is not a barrier between ourselves and God.
That is not what he means by a hidden God; a God whom
language hides from us. Rather, the notion of God in the lan-
guage we use is the notion of a hidden God, a *Deus absconditus*.
When Moelwyn Merchant tells us, 'Philosophy can provide him
with few definitions',[10] the remark can be misleading if we do not
see this is the rejection of *bad* philosophy. It cannot stand for the
rejection of philosophy as such, since there is a great deal in
contemporary philosophy of religion which emphasises that the
'grammar of God' is to be found in precisely the direction in
which R. S. Thomas's profoundest religious poems move. Moel-
wyn Merchant's conclusion leaves the poet somewhere *between*

faith and doubt, because he thinks 'God' is beyond conceptual truth. As we have seen, R. S. Thomas, tempted by such ideas, moves beyond them. Moelwyn Merchant, despite his conclusions, has to recognise that R. S. Thomas explored 'the language of negatives explored by the mystics'.[11] But is 'the language of negatives' a negative language? What we are concerned with here is the possibility of a *via negativa* in theology. To turn one's back on this possibility is nothing short of turning one's back on the task of mediating religious sense. When the poet insists that the search for a meaning which is beyond time must nevertheless take place in time, this is no trite truism. It is a reminder of the confusion involved in seeking to by-pass the mediation of religious sense by postponing it to a future, distant and more ethereal realm. R. S. Thomas insists that if talk of the eternal is to have any sense it must be mediated in the events, good and bad, which befall us. That is why the price is often a high one, and why our natural cries of distress can become a barrier to faith. The cry to God for those in peril on the sea, for example, is often conceived in terms of an attempt to avoid the peril. Such avoidance is, of course, a cause for rejoicing since it too comes from God. But the God of whom R. S. Thomas speaks is not a god who addresses himself only to the good things in life. On the contrary, it is of the essence of what he wants to say that God still speaks in great waters even when the perils are not removed and do their worst.

> You are there also
> at the foot of the precipice
> of water that was too steep
> for the drowned: their breath broke
> and they fell. You have made an altar
> out of the deck of the lost
> trawler whose spars
> are your cross. The sand crumbles
> like bread; the wine is
> the light quietly lying
> in its own chalice. There is
> a sacrament there more beauty
> than terror whose ministrant
> you are and the aisles are full
> of the sea shapes coming to its celebration.
>   ('In Great Waters', p. 114)

A sacrament that embraces beauty and terror can have a beauty of its own – that is what the poet–priest would celebrate in his verse. R. S. Thomas quotes Allen Tate's remark, 'Only persons of extraordinary courage and perhaps genius even can face the spiritual truth in its physical body.'[12] It is this courage which, as we have seen, characterises the deepest of R. S. Thomas's religious poems. He has already reminded us in 'Via Negativa',

> We look at people
> And places as though he had looked
> At them, too; but miss the reflection.
> ('Via Negativa', p. 23)

But to see the reflection is to look at people and things in a way which includes the light and the dark. It is to see them with the whole of existence as their background; to see them *sub specie aeternitatis*. J. R. Jones remarks, 'And you cannot see living things in this way, without blessing them, without gratitude for their existence, without profoundly thanking God for the miracle which made them, the miracle of their existence.'[13] He continues,

> insight into existence which makes us rejoice . . . is at the same time insight into its suffering, its defencelessness, its profound vulnerability . . . . It is not rare to feel this pity for those who are kindly disposed to you. The difficulty is to feel it for those who curse you or hate you or despitefully use you. Seeing in your enemy the profoundly pathetic, vulnerable, defenceless human being is the difficult thing . . . . Only love can *see* and where it sees it pities, irrespective of whether or not it receives pity in return. And that is why it 'beareth *all* things, suffereth *all* things'.[14]

Jones illustrates his point by reference to 'The Rime of the Ancient Mariner'. We remember the horrible consequences of the Mariner's killing the friendly albatross: how the ship was caught in a region of absolute calm under a withering sun:

> The very deep did rot: O Christ!
> That ever this should be!
> And slimy things did crawl with legs
> Upon the slimy sea.

As a terrible token of the Mariner's guilt the seamen 'slung the great rotting body of the bird round the Mariner's neck':[15]

> Instead of the cross, the Albatross
> About my head was hung.

All the crew die leaving the Mariner alone. He is in despair:

> Alone, alone, all all alone,
> Alone on that wide sea!
>
> I looked upon the rotting sea,
> And drew my eyes away;
> I looked upon the rotting deck,
> And there the dead men lay.
>
> I looked to Heaven, and tried to pray
> But or e'er prayer had gush't,
> A wicked whisper came, and made
> My heart as dry as dust.

But, suddenly, the Mariner begins to see things differently.

> Then in the silence under the blazing sun he began to look at what had earlier simply been an added loathsomeness – the slimy things which infested the water round the ship, and he began to be *aware* of them. . . . The swarming water-snakes suddenly seem to lie there with the whole world – the whole of existence – as their background. And this meant seeing them as they might be seen from Eternity. Something then welled up within him to which he could only give the name of 'love' and he *suddenly felt grateful for them* . . . gratitude for their existence. It is said in Genesis that 'God saw everything that he had made, and behold it was very good.' Sunk as he must have been in the depths of despair, it was something of this very fundamental experience that came to the Mariner; he saw existence objectively, as God might see it, and he saw it to be good. He gave thanks for it.[16]

> O happy living things! No tongue
> Their beauty might declare,

> A spring of love gushed from my heart
> And I blessed them unaware.
> Sure my kind saint took pity on me
> And I blessed them unaware.

The ability to bless is at the same time the losing of his burden:

> The self-same moment I could pray
> And from my neck so free
> The Albatross fell off and sank
> Like lead into the sea.

A sacrament which embraces beauty and terror – yet the poet knows that men cannot sustain such a celebration day in, day out. Terrors reassert their hold from time to time, and allegiance to the beautiful in the particular case naturally protests against them. At this level, there is much that is noble and true. Yet, the sacrament R. S. Thomas wants to celebrate attempts to transcend this context. This is why, at some point, something intrudes on the sacrament. Such intrusion has nothing to do with an alleged inevitable tension involved in trying to state something beyond conceptual truth (Merchant's suggestion). The intrusions are characteristic of what is often meant by the struggle of faith. It is in the context of such struggles that those who strive to celebrate the sacraments of their faith must, often, if they are honest, describe their situation as being 'betwixt and between'.

9   Betwixt and Between

At the end of Chapter 6, I called attention to the poems in R. S. Thomas's work which contain the deepest religious insights. These are made up of two poems in *Song at the Year's Turning*, one poem in *Poetry for Supper*, four poems in *Pietà*, and nine poems in *H'm*, the insights reaching maturity in this last volume. In the early volumes *The Stones of the Field* and *An Acre of Land*, it was the challenge to religious sense which dominated. And in volumes interspersed among these I have mentioned, in *The Minister*, *Tares*, *The Bread of Truth* and *Not that he Brought Flowers*, questions, difficulties and doubts reassert themselves. The struggle between belief and rebellion, between warring conceptions of God in *H'm* continues in *Laboratories of the Spirit*. The objections to certain ways of talking of God are expressed with an increased savagery, but in the poems 'Somewhere', 'The Moon in Lleyn', 'The Flower', 'Hill Christmas', 'The Prisoner', 'Farming Peter', 'The Bright Field', 'Llananno', 'Sea-Watching' and 'Alive', there is a return to the religious insights found in *H'm*. Yet, the poems which express difficulties for religion are just as powerful in *Laboratories of the Spirit* as those which express insights and, for many readers, they will no doubt make the greater impression. The volume *The Way of It* expresses these tensions too, but without the same measure of intensity.

As we have seen, in *Frequencies* the war between different ways of talking of God continues. Poems of great force are found on opposite sides of the tension. Poems which reassert and develop the deepest religious insights in previous volumes re-emerge: 'Play', 'The Answer', 'Perhaps', 'The Game', 'Adjustments', 'Emerging', 'The Small Country', 'Abercuawg' and 'In Great Waters'.

In picking out poems from the various volumes which contain the deepest religious insights my aim is not religious apologetic. Rather, it is simply to identify the character of the hard-won religious understanding in verse which R. S. Thomas has achieved.

132

Neither is it my intention to suggest that these poems are better works than those which express difficulties with and protests against other religious conceptions. I have tried to comment on striking poems from each side of the tension which the poet celebrates. Indeed, it is only over against the poems of protest and rebellion that the poems of religious affirmation can be fully appreciated.

In *H'm, The Laboratories of the Spirit* and *Frequencies*, as we have seen, there are magnificent evocations of the tensions to which I have referred. In the other volumes, it is the questioning or protesting voice which can be heard. Keeping in mind this oscillation of mood and spirit, it comes as no surprise to find that in *Between Here and Now* (1981) it is the question rather than the protest which dominates. Affirmation recedes. Yet, in the way the poet wrestles with his questions, he casts further light on the necessary conditions which must be met if there is to be a successful mediation of religious sense in language.

If there is one heresy which stands in the way of such media-tion it is the Manichean heresy – the belief that all matter is evil and that the infinite can be approached directly. What we have seen is that, if talk of the eternal is to have any sense, it must be seen in an illumination it provides or fails to provide for the temporal facts of human existence. This condition of intelligibil-ity is emphasised again and again in the questions which the poet puts to himself in *Between Here and Now*.

R. S. Thomas's volume is divided into two parts. In the first, each poem is a reaction to an impressionist painting in the Louvre. The second part, 'Other Poems', is, as I shall try to show, intimately connected with the most important issues raised in the first part. R. S. Thomas, alarmed at the increased difficulty of speaking of God, wonders whether, in his verse, something of the sense of doing so may be celebrated. It is instructive to approach R. S. Thomas's volume by recalling Keats's 'Ode on a Grecian Urn'. We remember how, for most of the poem, Keats describes scenes depicted on the urn; scenes which are celebrated there, but which are beyond all change.

> Ah, happy, happy boughs! that cannot shed
> Your leaves, nor ever bid the Spring adieu;
> And, happy melodist, unwearied,
> For ever piping songs for ever new;

> More happy love! more happy, happy love!
> For ever warm and still to be enjoy'd,
> For ever panting, and for ever young;

Such timelessness cannot belong to life itself, and only confusion results from wanting to freeze the transitory into timelessness.

> Thou, silent form, dost tease us out of thought
> As doth eternity: Cold Pastoral!
> When old age shall this generation waste,
> Thou shalt remain, in midst of other woe
> Than ours, a friend to man, to whom then say'st,
> 'Beauty is truth, truth beauty,' – that is all
> Ye know on earth, and all ye need to know.

The equation of beauty and truth is all the urn needs to know, since it does not have a human life to live. But for us, who have such lives to live, such equations cannot be made. It is instructive to place Keats's reference to boughs that cannot shed their leaves alongside Wallace Stevens's protest against the timelessness of one conception of a religious eternity:

> Is there no change of death in paradise?
> Does ripe fruit never fall? Or do the boughs
> Hang always heavy in that perfect sky?

Stevens finds a dignity in the very transitoriness of human life:

> Deer walk upon our mountains, and the quail
> Whistle about us their spontaneous cries;
> Sweet berries ripen in the wilderness;
> And, in the isolation of the sky,
> At evening, casual flocks of pigeons make
> Ambiguous undulations as they sink
> Downward to darkness, on extended wings.[1]

As we have seen, R. S. Thomas is no stranger to this mode of celebration. Its appeal is capable of reasserting its hold on him:

> Men who have hardly uncurled
> from their posture in the

womb. Naked. Heads bowed, not
in prayer, but in contemplation
of the earth they came from,
that suckled them on the brown
milk that builds bone not brain.

Who called them forth to walk
in the green light, their thoughts
on darkness? Their women,
who are not Madonnas, have babes
at the breast with the wise,
time-ridden faces of the Christ
child in a painting by a Florentine

master. The warriors prepare poison
with love's care for the Sebastians
of their arrows. They have no
God, but follow the contradictions
of a ritual that says
life must die that life
may go on. They wear flowers in their hair.
('Forest Dwellers', p. 153[2])

Why should people be required to be on their knees?

Heads bowed
over the entrails,
over the manuscript, the
block, over the rows
of swedes.

Do they never look up?
Why should one think
that to be on one's knees
is to pray?
The aim is to walk tall
in the sun.
('Rent')

On the other hand, there are those who do have a God. How is
their language to be understood? Can the act of kneeling be
dismissed so lightly?

> Two million years
> in straightening them
>   out, and they are still bent
> over the charts, the instruments,
>   the drawing board,
> the mathematical navel
>   that is the wink of God.
>   (p. 147)

Despite his comments, Keats calls the urn 'a friend to man'. His poem raises the issue of how the æsthetic completeness given in the urn is to speak to the ragged meadows men have to dwell in. Keats hints that similar issues can be raised about eternity. How are the eternal truths of religion to inform the changeableness of human life? Attempts to answer this question run the risk of 'teasing us out of thought'. As we have seen, R. S. Thomas recognises that there can be no neat fit between beauty and truth:

> One thing I have asked
> Of the disposer of the issues
> Of life: that truth should defer
> To beauty. It was not granted.
>   ('Petition', p. 12)

What is more, we have seen why such a petition, natural though it is, cannot be granted. We have seen that no divine plan can be inferred from the mixed character of things: that the will of God is inseparable from God's silence in such contexts. But how is this notion of the will of God to be understood?

In discussing this question in *Purity of Heart*, Kierkegaard brings out an analogy with the way in which the sea mirrors the heavens. Kierkegaard is concerned about the various ways in which worldliness can come between man's will and the will of God:

Purity of heart: it is a figure of speech that compares the heart to the sea, and why just to this? Simply for the reason that the depth of the sea determines its purity, and its purity determines its transparency. Since the sea is pure only when it is deep, and is transparent only when it is pure, as soon as it is impure, it is no longer deep but only surface water, and as soon as it is only surface water it is not transparent. When, on the contrary, it is deeply and transparently pure, then it is all of one consistency, no matter how long one looks at it; then its purity is this constancy in depth and transparency. On this account we compare the heart with the sea, because the purity of the sea lies in its constancy of depth and transparency. No storm may perturb it; no sudden gust of wind may stir its surface, no drowsy fog may sprawl out over it; no doubtful movement may stir within it; no swift-moving cloud may darken it: rather it must lie calm, transparent to its depths. And today if you should see it so, you would be drawn upwards by contemplating the purity of the sea. If you saw it every day, then you would declare that it is forever pure – like the heart of that man who wills but one thing. As the sea, when it lies calm and deeply transparent, yearns for heaven, so may the pure heart, when it is calm and deeply transparent, yearn for the Good. As the sea is made pure by yearning for heaven alone; so may the heart become pure by yearning only for the Good. As the sea mirrors the elevation of the heavens in its pure depths, so may the heart when it is calm and deeply transparent mirror the divine elevation of the Good in its pure depths. If the least thing comes in between, between the heavens and the sea, between the heart and the Good, then it would be sheer impatience to covet the reflection. For if the sea is impure it cannot give a pure reflection of the heavens.[3]

The ideal, then, according to Kierkegaard, is to have an unimpeded reflection of the heavens in the transparent sea. The human will ideally is simply to reflect the divine will. Unfortunately, the analogy limps. It depends on characterising the issue facing us as bringing two non-problematic notions into relation with each other, the will of man and the will of God. The real issue is to show how the notion of the will of God gets a hold on human life in the first place. As we have seen, the notion of God's will cannot be approached directly; its application in human life cannot be ignored, for it is in that context that its sense is to be found. And that context, the sea, *is* constantly disturbed. If human life is not an untroubled, transparent sea, but one troubled by storms, fogs, clouds and doubtful movements, what sense is there in saying that the heavens can be reflected in such circumstances? How can talk of God inform human life if the central features of that life are ignored?

As we have seen, this has been a central, if not the central concern in R. S. Thomas's poetry. In response to Jongkind's *The Beach at Sainte-Adresse*, the poet, realising that the painter desires a harmony in his painting between sea and sky, finds the harmony challenged by the intrusion of a boat, motionless in the sand; a boat which recalls the undeniable fact of human suffering.

> An agreement between
> land and sea, with both using
> the same tone? But the boat,
> motionless in the sand, refuses
>
> to endorse it, remembering
> the fury of the clawing
> of white hands. However skilfully
> the blue surface mirrors
>
> the sky, to the boat it is
> the glass lid of a coffin
> within which by cold lips
> the wooden carcases are mumbled.
>   ('Jongkind: *The Beach at Sainte-Adresse*'[4])

Is the sea a reflection of the heavens or the lid of a coffin which covers the lost souls? Certainly, for Thomas, religion cannot speak if it bypasses such suffering. It is the sea that worries the poet, the record of human misfortune, the tides in the affairs of men which make indecipherable marks on the shore:

> You ask why I don't write
> But what is there to say?
> The salt current swings in and out
> of the bay, as it has done
> time out of mind. How does that help?
> It leaves illegible writing
> on the shore. If you were here,
> we would quarrel about it.
> People file past this seascape

as ignorantly as through a gallery
of great art. I keep searching for meaning.
The waves are a moving staircase
to climb, but in thought only.
The fall from the top is as sheer
as ever. Younger I deemed truth
was to come at beyond the horizon.
Older I stay still and am
as far off as before. These nail-parings
bore you? They explain my silence.
I wish there were as simple
an explanation for the silence of God.
('Correspondence', p. 134)

The poet seems to have reverted to some of the earliest questions
he ever asked about the sense of human endurance. Yet, these
questions, in a more prosperous world, are not occasioned by the
harsh circumstances in which such endurance was shown. As we
have seen, Prytherch has gone. In his reaction to the train-
travellers in a Monet painting, the poet notes the new breed of
men he has to deal with. He is sceptical about the direction in
which they are travelling.

The passengers appear
to attest this, lingering
on, syringing their ears
with escaping steam
of the old sounds from the fields
that have accumulated there
over the centuries like wax.
('Monet: *The Gare Saint-Lazare*'[5])

Far more savage is his rejection of the materialism of the town
which makes it impossible to speak to God. The materialism is a
form of crucifixion.

They come in from the fields
with the dew and the buttercup dust
on their boots. It was not they
nor their ancestors crucified
Christ. They look up at what

the town has done to him,
hanging his body in stone on a stone
cross, as though to commemorate
the bringing of the divine beast
to bay and disabling him.

He is hung up high, but higher
are the cranes and scaffolding
of the future. And they stand by,
men from the past, whose role
is to assist in ·the destruction
of the past, bringing their own beasts
in to offer their blood up
on a shoddier altar.

                    The town
is malignant. It grows, and what
it feeds on is what these men call
their home. Is there praise
here? There is the noise of those
buying and selling and mortgaging
their conscience, while the stone
eyes look down tearlessly. There
is not even anger in them any more.
                    ('Fair Day', p. 137)

How can there be praise here? The poet would like to think that,
even if the surrounding circumstances change, there can still be
talk of God with sense in verse and art.

          Art is a sacrament
in itself. Now that
the angelus is silent

the brush-strokes go on
calling from the canvas's
airier belfries
to the celebration of colour.
     ('Gauguin: *The Alyscamps at Arles*'[6]).

There are moods in which the poet hopes to find a refuge from
time in art.

Art is recuperation
from time. I lie back
convalescing upon the prospect
of a harvest already at hand.
  ('Pissaro: *Kitchen Garden, Trees in Bloom*'[7])

He longs for the timelessness he finds in art to be part of life
itself. There is a danger of fantasy in his reaction to Pissaro's
Landscape at Chaponval.

It would be good to live
in this village with time
stationary and the clouds
going by. . . .
  ('Pissaro: *Landscape at Chaponval*'[8])

But these are moods, passing reactions. Many of them contain
contradictions. He wants time to be stationary, and yet he has to
acknowledge that the clouds pass by. The poet knows that art
itself is not immune from time. What the content of art is, and
how it is viewed, are themselves subject to historical and cultural
changes. For example, the formality of the group in Bazille's
Family Reunion, with their fine clothes dominating their natural
background under the trees, tells of an age and social possibili-
ties long gone:

Their looks challenge
us to find
    where they failed.

Well-dressed, well-
fed; their servants
    are out of sight,
snatching a moment
    to beget offspring
who are to overturn all this.
  ('Bazille: *Family Reunion*'[9])

But if these possibilities can disappear, what of religious possi-
bilities; is there not a possibility of these being overturned too?
Commenting on the woman outside the church in Van Gogh's
The Church at Auvers the poet says,

                    The
      woman is not going
      there. Though Catholic
      she is one of Herbert's
          people, who sweep
      rooms, scrub floors,
          down on their knees
      as the angelus rings
      out from an uncaring belfry
      ('Van Gogh: *The Church at Auvers*'[10])

The poet knows, as we have seen, that in order for the prayers on
our knees to mean anything they must inform those times in life
which bring us to our knees. It is these latter that have re-
emerged at the forefront of the poet's mind – the bleakness in
human life. Confronting the snow of Gaugin's Breton village, he
sees what is needed in face of such bleakness:

                  If prayers
      are said here, they are
      for a hand to roll
      back this white quilt
          and uncover the bed
      where the earth is asleep,
          too, but never awaking.
      ('Gauguin: *Breton Village in the Snow*'[11])

But what form can awaking take? If there have been changes in
men's attitudes and if misfortunes have befallen men, all of
which have made it difficult to see what religion has to say to
them, we have also seen that within religion itself certain re-
sponses are dumb in such circumstances. Are there religious
responses which are not silenced?

   In previous volumes R. S. Thomas has given us profound
religious answers to this question, but now it is the question
which dominates. In a culture in which the greatest respect is
accorded to truths which admit of factual verification, is there
any way of talking about God without being irrational?

      In the silence
      that is his chosen medium

of communication and telling
others about it
in words. Is there no way
not to be the sport
of reason? For me now
there is only the God-space
into which I send out
my probes. I had looked forward
to old age as a time
of quietness, a time to draw
my horizons about me,
to watch memories ripening
in the sunlight of a walled garden.
But there is the void
over my head and the distance
within that the tireless signals
come from. An astronaut
on impossible journeys
to the far side of the self
I return with messages
I cannot decipher, garrulous
about them, worrying the ear
of the passer-by, hot on his way
to the marriage of plain fact with plain fact.
('The New Mariner', p. 145)

In earlier volumes, the poet was able to show us how the radical
contingency of things, although militating against the gods of
theodicies, was actually a precondition for a different apprecia-
tion of a sense in which all things come from God. But now that
contingency seems to be an unsurmountable obstacle once more.

What is a galaxy's meaning?
The stars relay to the waste
places of the earth, as they do
to the towns, but it is
a cold message. There is randomness
at the centre, agitation subsisting
at the heart of what would be
endless peace.

> A man's shadow
> falls upon rocks that are
> millions of years old, and
> thought comes to drink at that dark
> pool, but goes away thirsty.
>   ('Senior', p. 143)

The poet is aware that some people claim to have success in calling on God, but he is not one of them:

> There was one being
> would not reply, God,
> I whispered, refining
> my technique, signalling
> to him on the frequencies
> I commanded. But always
> amid the air's garrulousness
> there was the one station
> that remained closed.
>   Was
> there an alternative
> medium? There were some claimed
> to be able to call him
> down to drink unsatiably
> at the dark sumps of blood.
>   ('One Way', p. 141)

Many of those who are confident about their communion with God seem to have a magical conception of what that communion is. We are introduced to unmediated conceptions of salvation, instant answers, such as those that doomed the minister and many of his congregation in *The Minister*. The poet sees that the religious ideas involved are too simple, cut off from the working-through in the ordinary details of life which genuine religious faith involves. Yet, although he rejects such simplicity, there is no ready alternative at hand for him.

> Yesterday a sinner,
> today fetching my soul
> from the divine laundry
> to wear it in the march past

tomorrow of the multitude
of white robes no man
can number?
                    Too simple.
There are girls, reversions,
the purse's incontinence.
Truth has its off-days,
too.
        Forgetting yesterday,
ignorant of the future,
I take up apartments
in the here and now, furnishing
them with my reflections,
renting them with each breath
I draw; staring from a window
without view in the spurious
silence of an electric clock.
                    ('Flat'[12])

If God is to have a word in time for the poet, he must address him where he is. The poet–priest is well aware of the various theological formulæ which have been used to talk of God, but they seem to have become a dead letter. Perhaps some of them could never have meant what they wanted to say. And so the poet describes the dilemma he finds himself in:

It was because there was nothing to do
that I did it; because silence was golden
I broke it. There was a vacuum
I found myself in, full of echoes
of dead languages. Where to turn
when there are no corners? In curved
space I kept on arriving
at my departures. I left no stones
unraised, but always wings
were tardy to start. In ante-rooms
of the spirit I suffered the anæsthetic
of time and come to with my hurt
unmended. Where are you? I
shouted, growing old in
the interval between here and now.
                    ('Pluperfect', p. 136)

How is the poet's predicament to be understood? It seems that
religious reactions are threatened; he no longer finds that they
come naturally to him, where 'naturally' does not mean 'easily'.
The central symbol of the Christian faith creates difficulties for
him.

> In this desert of language
>   we find ourselves in,
> with the sign-post with the word 'God'
>   worn away
>   and the distance . . . ?
>
> Pity the simpleton
>   with his mouth open crying:
>   How far is it to God?
>
> And the wiseacre says: Where you were,
> friend.
>   You know that smile
>   glossy
> as the machine that thinks it has outpaced
>   belief?
>   I am one of those
> who sees from the arms opened
>   to embrace the future
> the shadows of the Cross fall
>   on the smoothest of surfaces
>   causing me to stumble.
>   ('Directions', p. 131)

It is as if the poet–priest has to relearn the most primitive
religious responses. He cannot go back to the defiant attitudes of
his youth, but neither does he seem able to go forward.

> Yeats said that. Young
> I delighted in it:
> there was time enough.
>
> Fingers burned, heart
> scarred, a bad taste
> in the mouth, I read him

again, but without trust
any more. What counsel
has the pen's rhetoric

to impart? Break mirrors, stare
ghosts in the face, try
walking without crutches

at the grave's edge? Now
in the small hours
of belief the one eloquence

to master is that
of the bowed head, the bent
knee, waiting, as at the end

of a hard winter
for one flower to open
on the mind's tree of thorns.
('Waiting for It', p. 133)

This emphasis on lost primitive religious reactions, which I insist on, will annoy many philosophers. There is a powerful tradition in which the response to my insistence would be to say that responses are parasitic on belief. The problem, it will be said, is one not of religious responses, but of religious beliefs. Belief comes first as the reason and justification of our responses. This is a tradition in philosophy that needs to be undermined. If we ask ourselves what belief in God is divorced from any affective state or attitude, it will turn out to be an artificial construction of philosophy. Belief has sense only in the contexts of a wide range of reactions from devotion to rebellion. When the poet–priest talks of a crisis in such reactions, he is talking of a crisis of belief at the same time.

The point I am making has a wider application than religious belief. The term 'primitive reactions' and the discussion of it I borrow from the philosophical work of Ludwig Wittgenstein. One of the best accounts of what the term involves can be found in Norman Malcolm's article 'The Relation of Language to Instinctive Behaviour'.[13] Primitive reactions are, for example, instinctive reactions of pain, fear, surprise or desire. The emphasis in Wittgenstein is in direct opposition to the rationalistic assumption that speculation precedes action in the forming of our concepts. Wittgenstein says, 'Language did not emerge from reasoning.'[14] Malcolm comments,

> The idea is most plausible in respect to simple linguistic expressions of fear, pain, surprise, desire. A small child exhibits unlearned, instinctive, behaviour of fear. A dog rushes at it and it recoils with fear, just as a cat would. It would be absurd to attribute to either child or cat the thought, 'This beast may be dangerous, so I had better take avoiding action.'[15]

Similar reactions are involved in our recognition of pain in others. As Malcolm says, 'Plainly there are instinctive reactions of shock, concern, sympathy, when one sees that another person is injured.'[16] Primitive reactions feature in our reactions to heat and cold. Later, of course, more sophisticated and precise readings become possible. 'But', as Malcolm says, 'the thermometer would never have been taken to be a measure of heat and cold if there had not been a rough agreement between the contraction and expansion of mercury in a tube and the natural behavioural responses of human beings to heat and cold.'[17] Our interest in causal connections too begins in primitive reactions. Malcolm asks us to

> Suppose that a child runs into another child, knocking him down. The latter might react by leaping up and hitting or kicking the other one. . . . The child would not be doubting or wondering what made him fall. He would not want to observe what happens in other cases. Nor could he be said to *assume* that in similar cases the same thing occurs.[18]

Wittgenstein remarks,

> There is a reaction which can be called 'reacting to the cause'. – We also speak of 'tracing' the cause; a simple case would be, say, following a string to see who is pulling it. If I then find him – how did I know that he, his pulling, is the cause of the string's moving? Do I establish this by a series of experiments?[19]

Of these primitive reactions Wittgenstein says, 'The origin and the primitive form of the language-game is a reaction; only from this can the more complicated forms grow. Language – I want to say – is a refinement; "in the beginning was the deed".'[20]

In opposition to the rationalistic conception of concept formation, Wittgenstein makes *action* central. There is a striking similarity between this emphasis and one found in Simone Weil's account of concept formation. She says, 'The very nature of the relationship between ourselves and what is external to us, a relationship which consists in a reaction, a reflex, is our perception of the external world. Perception of nature, pure and simple, is a sort of dance, it is this dance that makes perception possible for us.'[21] As Peter Winch points out,

> Simeon Weil's account, like Wittgenstein's, achieves this by making the notion of *action* central. Action is conceived, in the first instance, as a series of bodily movements having a certain determinate temporal order. In its primitive form action is quite unreflective. Human beings, and other animate creatures, naturally react in characteristic ways to objects in their environments. They salivate in the presence of food and eat it; this already effects a rudimentary classification (which doesn't have to be based on any reflection) between 'food' and 'not food'. Our eyes scan objects and connect with other characteristic movements of our bodies, we sniff things (or sometimes hold our noses), we exhibit subtly different reactions to things we put into our mouths – corresponding to such tastes as 'sour', 'sweet', 'salty', etc. – and so on. These reactions are refined and developed as we mature; and some of these refinements and developments are responses to training by other human beings around us. A staircase is something to be climbed, a chair is something to be sat in: compare Wittgenstein's remark: 'It is part of the grammar of the word "chair" that this is what we call "to sit in a chair".'[22] As Simone Weil expresses it: 'everything that we see suggests some kind of movement'.[23]

Simone Weil's figure of the dance of the body is a striking one. It is in the primitive bodily reactions referred to that we have the beginnings of the concepts involved. We do not first believe sounds to be loud or quiet, colours to be light or dark, tastes to be sour or sweet, and *then* decide to react accordingly. Without the brute fact that we agree *in* our reactions there would be no concepts of loud and quiet, light or dark, sour or sweet.

These observations, so central in the examples we have discussed, are no less central in religion. There too they militate against the rationalistic assumptions that we first decide whether we believe there is a God, and then react accordingly. But here, too, the dance of the body is also the expression of the dance of the soul. What comes first, *must* come first, if belief is to mean anything, is mastery or resistance to the bowed head, the bent knee. Without this recognition, no flower will open on the mind's tree of thorns. Beyond primitive religious responses, there are all the refinements of religion and theology, but when these are severed from those reactions they soon become a dead letter. One can imagine developments taking place which are themselves confused or distorting. Think of reaching out as a primitive expression of desire. In the complexities of a relationship between a man and a woman, all sorts of developments may, of course, occur. Should some of these cause one of the people involved to break off the relationship, the other may be unable to find words or deed to express adequately anything which would save the situation. The person may be thrown back on the primitive reaction – reaching out, in this case, in vain, for the other. The developments may be such that they actually distort the primitive reaction, as when one person hangs on to the other in a gesture which half suggests that one could hold onto a relationship by holding onto the person; that the strength of the embrace could somehow make the relationship strong. The person in the 'small hours' of the relationship may do little more than reach out as the other departs.

Is not this the situation of the poet–priest in *Between Here and Now*? Recalling Simone Weil's figure of the dance of the body, is not what we see here, in the main, the dance of the poet, thrown back on the most primitive of his religious reactions – the reaching-out for God? We search in vain in this volume for poems which extend the number of those which reveal R. S. Thomas's deepest religious insights. True, there is reflection on a suffering God, but one unrelieved by the action of grace.

> I feel sometimes
>   we are his penance
> for having made us. He
> suffers in us and we partake
>   of his suffering . . . .

                        Often
        I think that there is no end
        to this torment and that the electricity
        that convulses us is the fire
                in which a god
        burns and is not consumed.
                        ('Covenant', p. 132)

The impression is of God and man as victims of an original
mistake. The issue remains the same: how can religious sense be
mediated given the facts about the lives of human beings? How
does God enter human discourse? In the most important relig-
ious poems in other volumes, the mediation, as we have seen, is
achieved via the notion of a *Deus absconditus*, and a dying-to-the-
self which is informed by Christ's Cross. Now the tension has
returned. Is the answer on this earth or is there a message from
eternity? The question has already taken an unpromising form
and there is a hint of regret in the suggestion that an answer may
involve a cross.

            Who to believe?
            The linnet sings bell-like,
            a tinkling music. It says life
            is contained here; is a jewel

            in a shell casket, lying
            among down. There is another
            voice, far out in space,
            whose persuasiveness is the distance

            from which it speaks. Divided
            mind, the message is always
            in two parts. Must it be
            on a cross it is made one?
                        ('Voices', p. 138)

If the message is one message, the sense of saying so is not
worked out in these verses. The last poem in *Between Here and
Now* is called 'Threshold' and its title seems a precise description
of the spiritual status shown in the poems. Faced with sufferings,
questions, alternatives, vulgarities, the poet is forced back onto

primitive religious reactions where, minimally, he reaches out for something, being unable to develop the gesture into a more satisfactory unity. In R. S. Thomas's closing poem we find a powerful depiction of this condition.

> I emerge from the mind's
> cave into the worse darkness
> outside, where things pass and
> the Lord is in none of them.
>
> I have heard the still, small voice
> and it was that of the bacteria
> demolishing my cosmos. I
> have lingered too long on
>
> this threshold, but where can I go?
> To look back is to lose the soul
> I was leading upward towards
> the light. To look forward? Ah,
>
> what balance is needed at
> the edges of such an abyss.
> I am alone on the surface
> of a turning planet. What
>
> to do but, like Michelangelo's
> Adam, put my hand
> out into unknown space,
> hoping for the reciprocating touch?
>   ('Threshold', p. 155)

10   A Sacrifice of Language?

In the course of this essay, we have been introduced to the religious conception of a *Deus absconditus*. As we saw, from being introduced to the notion in a few poems in *Song at the Year's Turning*, *Poetry for Supper* and *Pietà*, it reaches its maturity in a far greater number of poems in *H'm*, *Laboratories of the Spirit* and *Frequencies*. We have also witnessed in these, and other volumes, powerful expressions of protesting questions to religious faith. Many of these questions concern a God who is contingently hidden from us. He has plans and designs, which, while on earth, we cannot understand. They are hidden from us. The questions and difficulties which can be brought to bear on such a conception of God are, it seems to me, unanswerable. Many of R. S. Thomas's poems give powerful expression to these questions and difficulties. The God who is a *Deus absconditus* is not contingently hidden from us. Inscrutableness is part of our conception of God. The grace of God is internally related to our realisation of the radical contingency of human life.

Yet, as we have seen, the belief in a *Deus absconditus* also has difficulties: not intellectual difficulties, but the struggles which are involved in keeping hold of any deep faith. Belief in a *Deus absconditus* is invaded by a desire for a quasi-present God, a God whose existence can be felt, if not proved. Alternatively, the belief is invaded by belief in a hidden God of the other kind. Being forced to recognise that God is not an additional presence among others, refuge is taken in the supposition that God is present, only removed from us. These conceptions of God invade, in different ways, belief in a *Deus absconditus*. As we saw in the last chapter, it is the question mark which dominates the volume *Between Here and Now*. The same can be said of the 'New Poems' which complete the selection in *R. S. Thomas: Later Poems 1972–1982*.

What form does the question take? Throughout much of R. S. Thomas's poetry the questions which threaten religious faith

are framed from the harshness of life in close contact with
nature. In 'Country Church' in *The Stones of the Field*, we meet the
church with a slender frame. The poet tells us, 'no friendly God
has cautioned / The brimming tides of fescue for its sake'.[1] The
harshness, as we saw, was not only in nature, but also often
found in the character of the people. There is no need to rehearse
these facts at this stage. We also saw how, in an increasingly
large number of poems as the volumes progressed, the poet
achieved a mediation of religious sense in face of such harshness.
From the beginning, however, the poet is aware that the way of
life of which he sings in under threat. He has more in mind than
the increasing mechanisation of farming, problematic though
this is for him in many ways. His references to the machine,
however, have a wider reference. They include an encroaching
materialism and a growing dependence on a utilitarian techno-
logical culture. This is the destiny which has awaited Adam and
Eve. In 'Once' in *H'm* this destiny is predicted:

> I took your hand,
> Remembering you, and together,
> Confederates of the natural day,
> We went forth to meet the Machine.
> ('Once', p. 11[2])

In the 'New Poems' in *Later Poems 1972–1982*, we might say that
man's meeting with the machine has been fully realised. A
religious sense is mediated in man's meeting with nature, but is
there a successful mediation of such sense in man's meeting with
the machine? Witnessing such a meeting the poet is frank about
the effect it has on him:

> I have come to the borders
> of the understanding. Instruct
> me, God, whether to press
> onward or to draw back.
> ('Gradual')

The problem is not a childish naïvety, but the inadequacy of the
concepts at his disposal:

> Rather am I at one with those

minds, all of whose instruments
are beside the point of
their sharpness. I need a technique
other than that of physics

for registering the ubiquity
of your presence.

(p. 178)

Yet, despite the inappropriateness of scientific techniques in
discussing God, the prestige of these techniques in our culture
constitutes a threat of such discussion, in verse, and elsewhere.

Their laboratories shine
with a cold radiance,
leprosy to me who have watched them run
through the corridors of our culture
shaking the carillon
of their instruments at us
and crying: Unclean!

('Adagio', p. 177)

The tree of knowledge, for the invasion of which Adam was
expelled from Eden, has been invaded again. R. S. Thomas has
commented much earlier on 'the absurd arrogance of supposing
that we now stand at the zenith of human history as the final
judge, when actually we are the preservers of an age which is at
best unimaginative'.[3] The tree of science threatens Calvary's tree.
Man must shelter under some tree:

It is why,
some say, if there were no tree,
we would have to set one up
for us to linger under,
its drops falling on us as though to confirm
he has blood like ourselves.
We have set one up, but
of steel and so leafless that
he has taken himself
off out of the reach
of our transmitted prayers.

('The Tree', p. 187)

Not only is the possibility of a religious sense threatened, but there is also the danger of putting one's trust in science:

> What shall we do
> with the knowledge growing
> into a tree that to shelter
> under is to be lightning struck?
> ('It', p. 182)

What kingdom does science, given free rein, threaten to usher in?

> The ploughshares are beaten
> to guns and bombs. Daily we publish
> hurrying with it to and fro on steel
> wings, the good news of the kingdom.
> ('Gospel', p. 207)

We thought, since we created it, that we had the machine under our control, but we had mistaken and underestimated the resources of the adversary. From its infancy it becomes sovereign over the language of our nurseries. Its modes of thought have invaded other ways of speaking, the effect being in some cases, the religious, for example, to put them beyond the grasp which once reached them.

> It addressed
> objects, preferred its vocabulary
> to their own; grew eloquent
> before a resigned
> audience. It was fed
> speech and vomited
> it and was not reproved. . . .
>
> Need I go on? It survived
> its disasters; met fact
> with the mind's guile; forged
> for itself wings, missiles.
> Launched itself on a dark
> night through the nursery
> window into adult orbit
> out of the reach of gravity's control.
> ('Brother', p. 204)

The possibility of the extinction of human beings becomes a major preoccupation for the poet. It is in face of such possibility that the poet seeks a language that can still speak meaningfully of eternity.

> I see him as somebody's infant
>> once, recipient
>> of love's showers pouring
>>> unwanted.
> I see the halo over
>> him swelling
> to the nuclear cloud.
> Friend, I say,
> nursing him with my eyes
>> from the bone's
> cancer, since we are at death's
>> door, come in,
> let us peer at eternity
> through the cracks in each other's hearts.
>> ('Calles', p. 196)

The thirteen blackbirds who live in a garden have a world of their own, but are mildly irritated by man's presence. In Wallace Stevens's poem the importance of the birds in man's world is what is celebrated. For R. S. Thomas, the question is whether there is to be any place for man in the natural world. Yet, the birds recognise that man has problems which they do not.

> After we have stopped
> singing, the garden is disturbed
> by echoes; it is
> the man whistling, expecting
> everything to come to him.
>> ('Thirteen Blackbirds Look at a Man')

Man masters what comes naturally to the birds. But his mastery is problematic:

> We spread our
> wings, reticulating
> our air-space. A man stands
> under us and worries
> at his ability to do the same.

The birds are not troubled by talk of another world. Perhaps
that talk is misleading and should not be heard.

> When night comes
> like a visitor
> from outer space
> we stop our ears
> lest we should hear tell
> of the man in the
> moon.

But the question bothering the poet is the last one the poem
poses:

> Summer is
> at an end. The migrants
> depart. When they return
> in spring to the garden,
> will there be a man among them?
> (p. 174)

Has the summer of religion come to an end too? This question
hovers around a number of poems which discuss, in various
contexts, what sense can be made of the end of things. The sailor
whose voyages are over cannot make sense of the last days he has
to spend 'out of touch with the times'. Buried, what sense can the
poet make of the sailor's fate?

> And I,
> can I accept your voyages
> are done; that there is no tide
> high enough to float you off
> this mean shoal of plastic
> and trash? Six feet down,
> and the bone's anchor too
> heavy for your child spirit
> to haul on and be up and away?
> ('Salt', p. 159)

The times are out of touch with religion, the religion the poet has
known. His problem in verse is to show that religion is not out of

touch with the times. This is not to be confused with vulgar insistences on relevance which would simply make trash of religion. It is simply the recognition that *if* religion is to speak to men it must address the situation they find themselves in. In the context of the 'New Poems' it is impossible to read the poet's depiction of the plight of grandparents without being conscious of the echoes it has in these wider contexts. This is achieved, not by turning the grandparents into symbols, but by the kind of attention the poet pays to their predicament.

> With the deterioration of sight
> they see more clearly what is missing
> from their expressions. With the
> dulling of the ear, the silences
> before the endearments are
> louder than ever. Their hands have their accidents
> still, but no hospital will
> receive them. With their licences
> expired, though they keep to their own
> side, there are corners
> in waiting. Theirs is a strange
> house. Over the door in
> invisible letters there is the name:
> Home, but it is no place
> to return to. On the floor
> are the upset smiles, on the
> table the cups unwashed they drank
> their happiness from. There are themselves
> at the windows, faces staring
> at an unreached finishing
> post. There is the sound
> in the silence of the breathing
> of their reluctant bodies as
> they enter each of them the last lap.
>
> ('Grandparents', p. 189)

Faced with the earlier challenges of the harshness of the natural world, the poet found a sense which depended on a celebration made possible even when plans and projects failed. The celebratory rite depended on an acceptance of things as God's gift, an acceptance which transcended success and failure

by embracing them. In the present volume, there is a poem
which recalls such a celebration. The poet suddenly comes upon
a village in the Welsh hills:

> A bird chimes
>   from a green tree
> the hour that is no hour
>   you know. The river dawdles
> to hold a mirror for you
> where you may see yourself
>   as you are, a traveller
>   with the moon's halo
> above him, who has arrived
> after long journeying where he
>   began, catching this
>   one truth by surprise
> that there is everything to look forward to.
>   ('Suddenly', p. 203)

The wheel has certainly turned full circle in this poem, but it is
significant that it is the old setting which affords the opportunity
for an emergence of sense. But can the poet reach the same one
truth in the new situation which faces him? In 'Farming Peter' in
Laboratories of the Spirit, no attention was paid to those who
reached to the Christ–scarecrow figure by saying that the
Saviour's face was made of straw. But the female scarecrow in
'New Poems' has a style which, though defiant, lacks content:

> She has an air about her
>   which more than makes up
> for her loss of face.
>
> There is nothing between us.
>   If I take her arm
> there is nowhere to go.
>
> We are alone and strollers
>   of a fine day with
> under us the earth's fathoms waiting.
>   ('Strays', p. 181)

There is an obvious diminishing of the religious perspective. There are still those in Wales who, like Moses, claim to have extraordinary religious experiences. The poet respects, but cannot embrace them.

> I have put off
> pride and, knowing the ground
> holy, lingered to wonder
> how it is that I do not burn
> and yet am consumed.
>
> ('The Bush')

The religious perspective he remembers is not what he sees now.

> And in this country
> of failure, the rain
> falling out of a black
> cloud in gold pieces there
> are none to gather,
> I have thought often
> of the fountain of my people
> that played beautifully here
> once in the sun's light
> like a tree undressing.
>
> (p. 194)

But how far back does the trouble go? Was the conception of God which became dominant in Christianity one which brought us to our present plight, a dominance itself rooted in a divorce between man and nature? In the primeval perspective there is little to celebrate:

> Such sounds
> as there were came from the strong
> torn by the stronger. The dawn tilted
> an unpolished mirror for the runt mind
> to look at itself in without recognition.
>
> ('Perspectives')

But this desire for conquest remains in man and is already the cause for regret in the neolithic perspective where an older form of religion is said to be in decline. In this context, the poet uses language which parallels that in which people today hope for a revival, but he thinks such hopes fail to penetrate to the root of the problem. He prophesies that a need will be felt to return to a religion which has an affinity with living things; one which does not depend on mastery over them.

> Some think
> there will be a revival.
> I don't believe it. This
> plucked music has come
> to stay. The natural breathing
> of the pipes was to
> a different god. Imagine
> depending on the intestines
> of a polecat for accompaniment
> to one's worship! I have
> attended at the sacrifice
> of the language that is the liturgy
> the priests like, and felt
> the draught that was God
> leaving. I think some day
> there will be nothing left
> but to go back to the place
> I came from and wrap
> myself in the memory
> of how I was young
> once and under the covenant
> of that God not given to folly.

But does it make sense for us to speak of a going-back, and, even if it does, would we not need more than memories to wrap ourselves in? Is there not a contradiction at the heart of the Christian eucharist? Is it not an attempt to gain forgiveness for a violence which is at variance with it? Is there violence and ambivalence, as Freud suggested, in the broken body and the spilt blood of the Christian perspective?

> Their dry bread
> broke like a bone.
> Wine in the cup

was a blood-stained mirror
for sinners to look
into with one eye
closed, and see themselves forgiven.

Men went forth to convert by the sword. The poet testifies,

I was my lord's bard,
telling again sweetly
what had been done bloodily.

The fruitlessness of the enterprises did not deter the conception
of 'bringing the true faith' embodied in them:

We made a brave foray;
the engagement was furious.
We came back alone. . . .

To-morrow, he promised,
we will ride forth again.

What of the modern perspective? The poet speaks of the power
station at Dinorwig in North Wales, contrasting it with the
natural surroundings. The slate quarries had begun the invasion
of nature:

And the brittle gardens
of Dinorwig, deep
in the fallen petals
of their slate flowers: such the autumn

of a people!

The poet asks what new perspective lies in store for us. There are
echoes of Yeats's beast 'slouching towards Bethlehem to be
born'.

Whose spring
is it sleeps in a glass
bulb, ready to astonish us
with its brilliance? Bring

> on the dancing girls
> of the future, the swaying
> pylons with their metal
> hair bickering towards England.
>   (p. 166)

And so the poet returns to his confrontation with the machine; a confrontation in which the machine is supremely confident of the surrender of language it will bring about in the poet.

>   Ice
>   in your veins, the poet
>   taunted; the life in you
>   ticking away; your breath
>   poison. I took him apart
>   verse by verse, turning
>   on him my x-ray
>   eyes to expose the emptiness
>   of his interiors. In houses
>   with no hearth he huddles
>   against me now, mortgaging
>   his dwindling techniques
>   for the amenities I offer.
>   ('The Other', p. 180)

But what of the *Deus absconditus*, the idea of God forged at such cost in earlier volumes? It, too, seems to be under siege.

>   Is absence enough?
>   I asked from my absent place
>   by love's fire. What god,
>   fingers in its ears, leered at me
>   from above the lintel, face
>   worn by the lapping
>   of too much time?
>   ('Cadenza')

The silence which, in previous poems, has been used as a purifying atheism, a purge of wrong answers in religion, now seems to turn on the notion of a *Deus absconditus* itself.

> I supposed, watching
> the starry equations,
> his thinking was done
> in a great silence; yet after
> he goes out, following
> himself into oblivion,
> the memory of him must smoke
> on in this ash, waiting
> for the believing people
> to blow on it. So some say
> were the stars born. So,
> say I, are those sparks
> forged that are knocked like nails
> one by one into the usurping flesh.
>   (p. 185)

The silences ask for the religious response which the poet has been able to make earlier in his verse. But that response seems to have become problematic. To perform it seems to involve a conjuring-trick, a sleight-of-hand, which the mind rejects. This is not the intellectual and moral rejection of the God of theodicies. Rather, it is asking a hidden God whether belief in him forces us to ignore too much.

> You do yourself
> harm, coming to us
> with your sleeves rolled up
>   as though not responsible
> for deception. We have seen
> you lay life like a cloth
>   over the bones
> at our parties and wave
>   your cold wand and expect
> us to smile, when you took it away
>   again and there was nothing.
>   ('Sleight', p. 195)

Are there no attempts to convey anything more positive for religious belief in the 'New Poems'? Very few, it seems. In speaking of Jesus and Paul it is the impression of pervasive misunderstanding rather than understanding which predominates. Did those who listened to Jesus understand him?

He wore no hat, but he produced, say
from up his sleeve, an answer
to their question about
the next life. It is here,
he said, tapping his forehead
as one would to indicate
an idiot. The crowd frowned

and took up stones
to punish his adultery
with the truth. But he, stooping
to write on the ground, looked
sideways at them, as they withdrew
each to the glass-house of his own mind.
                              ('Covenanters')

Do we understand Paul? Is it clear that Jesus would have been
happy with Paul's conclusions?

          Still, you are the mountain
the teaching of the carpenter of Nazareth
congealed into. The theologians
have walked round you for centuries
and none of them scaled you. Your letters remain
unanswered, but survive the recipients
of them. And we, pottering among the foot-hills
of their logic, find ourselves staring
across deep crevices at conclusions at which
the living Jesus would not willingly have arrived.
                              (p. 170)

But *what* has survived? A written text no doubt, although trans-
lation may threaten even that. But how is its meaning to be
mediated? That is determined by the significance the text has in
the lives of the people who use it. But those lives have changed.
What can religion mean in a Benthamite culture dominated by
the machine? So much the poet has celebrated seems to be
reduced to silence. Yet in the middle of the cluster of poems
which proclaim this fact is one which stands out sharply from
them. It is a poem which purports to celebrate God speaking to
man, even through the machine. I do not say that a mediation of

religious sense in such a context is impossible, but I do say there are difficulties in this poem. If read in relation to the deepest religious poems which have preceded it in earlier collections, it can be sustained by them, as was the poem 'Alive' in *Laboratories of the Spirit*. If, on the other hand, the poem is read in relation to those in the present volume which express concern about the influence of the machine, its language seems isolated and disconnected. The problem is that, up to now, the poet has not shown how, if at all, religious sense can be mediated in relation to the machine. Thus we have not seen how the machine too tells of God.

> Suddenly after long silence
> he has become voluble.
> He addresses me from a myriad
> directions with the fluency
> of water, the articulateness
> of green leaves; and in the genes,
> too, the components
> of my existence. The rock,
> so long speechless, is the library
> of his poetry. He sings to me
> in the chain-saw, writes
> with the surgeon's hand
> on the skin's parchment messages
> of healing. The weather
> is his mind's turbine
> driving the earth's bulk round
> and around on its remedial
> journey. I have no need
> to despair; as at
> some second Pentecost
> of a Gentile, I listen to the things
> round me: weeds, stones, instruments,
> the machine itself, all
> speaking to me in the vernacular
> of the purposes of One who is.
>   ('Suddenly', p. 201)

But what form does the speaking take in relation to the machine? Unlike the emergence of a *Deus absconditus* in the earlier poems,

where one saw how hard-fought such emergence was and noted
what was rejected on the way, here the significance of renewed
speech, in relation to the machine, is asserted, but not shown.
For example, there is nothing in the poem to say how we should
take the reference to God's purpose. Are we back with the God of
theodicies and all the difficulties such a conception involves?

The prevailing mood of the 'New Poems' is certainly not the
attempted expansiveness of 'Suddenly'. The mood is partly one
of a poet who knows that, having to tell of God in a world of
shifting and conflicting aspects, the ensuing verse, to be authen-
tic, must often testify to an indecision separated from grace:

> Here for a while heard
> voices powerless
> to obey looked fear
> in the face was outstared
> by it took lust
> for love burned more
> than his fingers saw need
> lie dropped it a tear
> passed on. Visitors
> from a far country
> beauty addressed him
> truth too he was no
> linguist keeping his balance
> without grace took
> one step forward and one
> back on the shining tightrope
> between dark and dark.
>   ('Citizen', p. 209)

The mood is also of a poet still determined to think, even if he
has to go on his knees to do so. He has suffered the rigidity of old
ideas which cannot accommodate the fire of faith. Nevertheless,
although the possibilities for mediating a religious sense may
diminish, the poet labours on with his struggle to achieve a
religious syntax in verse.

> Examine
> me, tap with your words'
> hammer, awaken memories

of fire. It is so long
since I cooled. Inside me,
stalactite and stalagmite,
ideas have formed and become
rigid. To the crowd
I am all outside.
To the pot-holing few there is a way
in along passages that become
narrower and narrower,
that lead to the chamber
too low to stand up in,
where the breath condenses
to the cold and locationless
cloud we call truth. It
is where I think.

('Inside', p. 199)

The passages by which truth must be sought are narrower and
narrower because the world which now awaits the mediation of
religious sense is one which is increasingly resistant to it. R. S.
Thomas realises that 'the attempt of contemporary Christianity
to be reasonable in faces of science makes it so innocuous . . .
and less capable of sustaining that creative tension of the intel-
lect and the emotions out of which the good life and the good
poem can be born'.[4] The poem which brings his collection to a
close expresses his prayer, as a poet, that he will be able to
celebrate the sense of eternity in verse. He realises too, however,
that, confronted by the fruits of the tree of science, he has not
been successful in doing so in this context. Like Baudelaire, he
too sees poetry as the effort to turn base metal into gold. But how
is this to be done at the present time where religious sense is
concerned? As we have seen, much of R. S. Thomas's poetry has
been concerned with the relation between Eden's tree of the
knowledge of good and evil and Calvary's tree – that relation, in
earlier poems, was discussed in relation to those trees and fields
among which the farmer works. A hard-won sense of a *Deus
absconditus* emerged in that context. But now Calvary's tree is
confronted by the tree of the knowledge which science brings.
Like Baudelaire, the poet cannot deny the fruit of this tree, but
R. S. Thomas wants to show how it, too, could speak of God. He

seems to admit that, as yet, he has not succeeded, as he did in the
earlier context of the world of his farmer, in showing how this is
possible.

> Baudelaire's grave
> not too far
> from the tree of science.
> Mine, too,
> since I sought and failed
> to steal from it,
> somewhere within sight
> of the tree of poetry
> that is eternity wearing
> the green leaves of time.
> ('Prayers', p. 214[5])

Yet, the poet has no choice. He too has his tree on which he must
continue to work. Earlier, in his profoundest religious poems,
R. S. Thomas showed us a God who only speaks when we learn
from the silence which confronts our misconceived questions.
But now people wonder whether the silence is expressive of God.
What if it is mere silence?

> Prepare yourself for the message.
> You are prepared?
>   Silence.
> Silence is the message.
> The message is . . . Wait.
> Are you sure? An echo?
> An echo of an echo?
>   Sound.
> Was it always there
>   with us failing
> to hear it?
>   What was the shell doing
> on the shore? An ear endlessly
>   drinking?
>   What? Sound? Silence?
> Which came first?
>   Listen.

I'll tell you a story
as it was told me by the teller
                    of stories.
Where did he hear it?
By listening? To silence? To sound?
            To an echo? To an echo
                    of an echo?
                        Wait.

('Questions', p. 193)

In the poems in which God is shown speaking in the silence which meets our misguided questions, the silence is characterised as a purificatory rite. Such a rite, involving, as it does, a purifying atheism, creates the condition by which wonder, praise, and the notion of God, can come in at the right place. That possibility seems to have receded in the world in which the poet now finds himself. He is hard put to celebrate the sense of faith in verse. But he does not abandon faith either. Not for the first time, the poet knows what he has to do: he has to wait.

When R. S. Thomas retired, he went to live at Porth Neigwl, a few miles from Aberdaron. The English name for the locality is Hell's Mouth. He is reported to have said, 'I have retired now, and I'm living at the Mouth of Hell.'[6] Remember, however, that R. S. Thomas has also said, 'The ability to be in hell is a spiritual prerogative.'[7] In his pilgrimage in verse, the poet has shown us a road to God which cannot by-pass the cry from the Cross: *Eli, Eli, lama sabachthani?*

Notes

NOTES ON THE INTRODUCTION

1. These issues were my preoccupation in a collection of essays, *Through a Darkening Glass* (Indiana: University of Notre Dame Press; Oxford: Basil Blackwell, 1982).
2. D. Z. Phillips, *Dramau Gwenlyn Parry* (Caernarvon: Pantycelyn Press, 1982).
3. In *Poetry for Supper* (London: Rupert Hart-Davis, 1958) p. 31. This powerful poem does not survive the selection in R. S. Thomas's *Selected Poems 1946–1968* (London: Rupert Hart-Davis, 1973; repr. London: Granada, 1983). The poem quoted from will be indicated at the initial quotation. All subsequent quotations are from the same poem until otherwise indicated.
4. 'Seeking the Poem in the Pain', in *Through a Darkening Glass*, pp. 189–90.
5. R. George Thomas, review of *H'm* in *Poetry Wales*, Spring 1972, p. 88. This whole number of *Poetry Wales* is devoted to a discussion of R. S. Thomas's work.
6. *A Choice of George Herbert's Verse*, selected with an introduction by R. S. Thomas (London: Faber and Faber, 1967) p. 12.
7. Ibid., p. 16.
8. John Mole, 'Signals from the Periphery', in *Critical Writings on R. S. Thomas*, ed. Sandra Anstey (Bridgend: Poetry Wales Press, 1982) p. 133. The interview referred to here was broadcast on BBC Radio 3 on 3 Jan 1975, under the title 'More Poetry at Large 4'.
9. *The Penguin Book of Religious Verse*, ed. with an introduction by R. S. Thomas (Harmondsworth: Penguin, 1963).
10. 'R. S. Thomas: Priest and Poet', transcript of John Ormond's film for BBC television, broadcast on 2 Apr 1972, in *Poetry Wales*, Spring 1972, p. 51.
11. Simone Weil, 'Draft for a Statement of Human Obligations' (1943), in *Selected Essays 1934–1943*, trs. Richard Rees (London: Oxford University Press, 1962).
12. M. O'C. Drury, 'Some Notes on Conversations with Wittgenstein', in *Ludwig Wittgenstein – Personal Recollections*, ed. Rush Rhees (Oxford: Basil Blackwell, 1981) p. 99.

13. Simone Weil, *First and Last Notebooks* (London: Oxford University Press, 1970) p. 147.
14. R. S. Thomas, 'A Frame for Poetry', *Times Literary Supplement*, 3 Mar 1966, p. 169.

NOTES TO CHAPTER 1: GESTURES AND CHALLENGES

1. W. Moelwyn Merchant, *R. S. Thomas*, Writers of Wales (Cardiff: University of Wales Press, 1979) p. 3.
2. 'R. S. Thomas: Priest and Poet', *Poetry Wales*, Spring 1972, p. 49.
3. In *Song at the Year's Turning* (London: Rupert Hart-Davis, 1955) p. 18. All verse quotations in this chapter are from this collection unless otherwise indicated.
4. *Selected Poems 1946–1968* (London: Granada, 1983) p. 3.
5. Merchant, *R. S. Thomas*, p. 9.
6. For a perceptive analysis 'of evasion, of self deception, of romantic posturing' in the poem see James A. Davies, 'Participating Readers: Three Poems by R. S. Thomas', *Poetry Wales*, XVIII, no. 4 (1983).
7. Merchant, *R. S. Thomas*, pp. 13–14.
8. T. S. Eliot, *The Idea of a Christian Society* (London: Faber and Faber, 1982) pp. 80–1.

NOTES TO CHAPTER 2: EARTH TO EARTH

1. In *Song at the Year's Turning*, p. 46. All verse quotations in this chapter are from this collection unless otherwise indicated.
2. See 'The Gap in the Hedge', ibid., p. 53.
3. Sigmund Freud, *The Future of an Illusion* (London: Hogarth Press, 1962) p. 46.
4. In *Selected Poems 1946–1968*, p. 10.
5. Roland Mathias, 'Philosophy and Religion in the Poetry of R. S. Thomas', *Poetry Wales*, Spring 1972, p. 40.
6. In *Selected Poems 1946–1968*, p. 11.
7. Ibid., p. 35.
8. 'Lament for Prytherch', in *Song at the Year's Turning*, p. 99.
9. John Ackerman, 'Man and Nature in the Poetry of R. S. Thomas', *Poetry Wales*, Spring 1972, p. 19.
10. In *Selected Poems 1946–1968*, p. 39.
11. Ibid., p. 34.

12. Cf. D. Z. Phillips, *The Concept of Prayer* (Oxford: Basil Blackwell, 1981) pp. 61–2, 98–100, 155–6.
13. In *Selected Poems 1946–1968*, p. 36.
14. Ibid., p. 42.
15. Ibid., p. 43.

NOTES TO CHAPTER 3: TESTING THE SPIRITS

1. Merchant, *R. S. Thomas*, p. 29.
2. In *Selected Poems 1946–1968*. Page references following quotations from *The Minister* refer to this collection.
3. See the discussion of 'Soil' in Chapter 2.
4. Søren Kierkegaard, *Purity of Heart*, trs. Douglas Steere (New York: Harper Torchbooks, 1956).
5. Cf. D. Z. Phillips, 'Knowledge, Patience and Faust', in *Through a Darkening Glass*, p. 105.
6. Flannery O'Connor, *Mystery and Manners*, selected and ed. Sally and Robert Fitzgerald (New York: Farrar, Straus and Giroux, 1969) p. 69.
7. Ibid., pp. 161–2.
8. R. S. Thomas, 'A Frame for Poetry', *Times Literary Supplement*, 3 Mar 1966, p. 169.

NOTES TO CHAPTER 4: AN INADEQUATE LANGUAGE?

1. In *Poetry for Supper* (London: Rupert Hart-Davis). All verse quotations in this section are from this collection unless otherwise indicated.
2. In *Selected Poems 1946–1968*, p. 55.
3. Merchant, *R. S. Thomas*, p. 42.
4. Ibid., p. 43.
5. While also rejecting Merchant's reading of the poem, James A. Davies misses what I take to be the unsavoury character of the hope expressed at the climax of the poem. He says that to 'the final insistence upon eventual divine reward . . . the demoralised narrator is wholly and depressingly indifferent' ('Participating Readers', *Poetry Wales*, XVIII, no. 4, p. 82). To me, it is the character of his concern that is worrying.
6. In *Selected Poems 1946–1968*, p. 47.
7. Ibid., p. 57.
8. Ibid., p. 51.

9. Ibid., p. 56.
10. Ibid., p. 53.
11. In *Tares* (London: Rupert Hart-Davis, 1961). All verse quotations in this section are from this collection unless otherwise indicated.
12. In *Selected Poems 1946–1968*, p. 63.
13. Ibid., p. 68.
14. In *The Bread of Truth* (London: Rupert Hart-Davis, 1963). All verse quotations in this section are from this collection unless otherwise indicated.
15. In *Selected Poems 1946–1968*, p. 89.
16. Merchant, *R. S. Thomas*, p. 68.
17. A. E. Dyson, *Yeats, Eliot and R. S. Thomas* (London: Macmillan, 1981) p. 302.
18. Benedict Nightingale, 'Hewer of Verses', in *Critical Writings on R. S. Thomas*, ed. Sandra Anstey (Bridgend: Poetry Wales Press, 1982) p. 35.
19. John Ackerman, 'Man and Nature in the Poetry of R. S. Thomas', *Poetry Wales*, Spring 1972, p. 15.
20. Robert Mathias, 'Philosophy and Religion in the Poetry of R. S. Thomas', ibid., p. 28.

NOTES TO CHAPTER 5: WAITING FOR GOD

1. Mathias, 'Philosophy and Religion in the Poetry of R. S. Thomas', *Poetry Wales*, Spring 1972, p. 44.
2. In *Pietà* (London: Rupert Hart-Davis, 1966). All quotations in the first part of this chapter are from this collection unless otherwise indicated.
3. In *Selected Poems 1946–1968*, p. 98.
4. Ibid., pp. 102–3.
5. 'R. S. Thomas: Priest and Poet', a transcript of John Ormond's 1972 BBC film, in *Poetry Wales*, Spring 1972, p. 50.
6. In *Selected Poems 1946–1968*, p. 99.
7. Ibid., p. 100.
8. Ibid., p. 104.
9. Ibid., p. 97.
10. Ibid., p. 93.
11. Ibid., p. 129.
12. Ibid., p. 109.
13. Ibid., p. 123.
14. Anthony Conran, 'R. S. Thomas and the Anglo-Welsh Crisis', *Poetry Wales*, Spring 1972, p. 72.
15. In *Selected Poems 1946–1968*, p. 114.
16. In *Not that he Brought Flowers* (London: Rupert Hart-Davis, 1968).

17. Ibid., p. 40.
18. In *Selected Poems 1946–1968*, p. 113.
19. Ibid., p. 110.
20. In *Not that he Brought Flowers*, p. 16.
21. In *Selected Poems 1946–1968*, p. 118.
22. Ibid., p. 119.
23. Sam Adams, 'A Note on Four Poems', *Poetry Wales*, Spring 1972, p. 79.
24. 'R. S. Thomas, Priest and Poet', a transcript of John Ormond's BBC film, ibid., p. 51.
25. For a discussion of such confused conclusions, see my discussion of Martin Esslin's views of Beckett's conception of 'waiting' in *Waiting for Godot*, in 'Meaning, Memory and Longing' in *Through a Darkening Glass*.
26. Adams, 'A Note on Four Poems', *Poetry Wales*, Spring 1972.

NOTES TO CHAPTER 6: GOD'S REFLECTIONS

1. Dyson, *Yeats, Eliot and R. S. Thomas*, p. 305.
2. In *Young and Old* (London: Chatto and Windus, 1972) p. 25.
3. Hume, *Dialogues Concerning Natural Religion*, p. 211.
4. In *Later Poems 1972–1982* (London: Macmillan, 1983). All verse quotations in this chapter are from this collection unless otherwise indicated.
5. In *H'm* (London: Macmillan, 1972) p. 21.
6. Hume, *Dialogues Concerning Natural Religion*, p. 169.
7. In *H'm*, p. 5.
8. Brian Morris, 'The Topography of R. S. Thomas', in *Critical Writings on R. S. Thomas*, p. 151.
9. In *H'm*, p. 26.
10. Ibid., p. 17.
11. Kierkegaard, *Purity of Heart*, pp. 171–2.
12. Ibid., p. 173.
13. Ibid., p. 173.
14. Ibid., p. 174.
15. Ibid.
16. Peter Winch, 'Can a Good Man be Harmed?', in *Ethics and Action* (London: Routledge and Kegan Paul, 1972) p. 206.
17. Simone Weil, *Waiting on God*, trs. Emma Craufurd (London: Fontana, 1959) p. 173.
18. Flannery O'Connor, 'A Good Man is Hard to Find', in her collection of the same title (London: Faber and Faber, 1968).
19. 'R. S. Thomas: Priest and Poet', in *Poetry Wales*, Spring 1972, p. 56.

20. Kierkegaard, *Purity of Heart*, pp. 106–7.
21. Dyson, *Yeats, Eliot and R. S. Thomas*, p. 309.
22. A comment made to and reported in Timothy Wilson, 'R. S. Thomas', in *Critical Writings on R. S. Thomas*, p. 67.

NOTES TO CHAPTER 7: PRESENCE AND ABSENCE

1. R. S. Thomas, *Abercuawg* (Llandysul: Gomer Press, 1976) p. 5: 'Lle mae Abercuawg? Nid wy'n sicr ai dyna'r ffordd iawn i ofyn y cwestiwn. 'Rwy'n rhyw hanner ofni mai'r ateb i hwnnw ydyw nad' ydyw'n bod o gwbl. Ac fel Cymro ni welaf ystyr i'm bywyd os nad oes y fath le ag Abercuawg, tref neu bentref y mae'r cogau'n canu ynddo.'
2. Ibid., p. 16: 'Nid yw'r ffaith ein bod ni'n mynd i ardal Machynlleth i chwilio am safle Abercuawg a dweud: "Na, nid hon ydyw hi", yn golygu dim. Nid testun siom ac anobaith sydd yma, ond ffordd i gael gwybod yn well, trwy ei absenoldeb, natur y lle yr ydym yn chwilio amdano.'
   For a collection of R. S. Thomas's prose and translations of some of his Welsh essays, see *R. S. Thomas Selected Prose*, ed. Sandra Anstey, introduction by Ned Thomas (Bridgend: Poetry Wales Press, 1983).
3. Ibid., p. 17: the English translation in this instance is by Moelwyn Merchant, *op. cit.*, p. 80. 'Dyma ystad dyn. Y mae ef bob amser ar fedr angyffred Duw; ond yn gymaint â'i fod yn greadur ac yn feidrol, ni wna byth. 'Wêl ef byth mo Abercuawg ychwaith. Ond trwy geiso ei gweld, trwy hiraethu andani, trwy wrthod derbyn ei bod yn perthyn i'r gorffennol, a'i bod wedi mynd i ebargofiant; trwy wrthod derbyn rhywbeth ail-law yn ei lle hi, fe lwydda i'w chadw hi fel posibilrwydd tragwyddol.'
4. Simone Weil, *First and Last Notebooks* (London: Oxford University Press, 1970) p. 147.
5. In *Later Poems 1972–1982*. All verse quotations in this chapter are from this collection unless otherwise indicated.
6. Dyson, *Yeats, Eliot and R. S. Thomas*, p. 315.
7. Ibid., p. 314.
8. In *Laboratories of the Spirit* (London: Macmillan, 1975) p. 50.
9. Phillips, 'Seeking the Poem in the Pain', in *Through a Darkening Glass*, p. 187.
10. Randal Jenkins, 'R. S. Thomas: Occasional Prose', in *Critical Writings on R. S. Thomas*, p. 75.
11. *Selected Poems of Edward Thomas*, selected with an introduction by R. S. Thomas (London: Faber and Faber, 1964) p. 11.

12. Phillips, 'Seeking the Poem in the Pain', in *Through a Darkening Glass*, p. 188.
13. Ibid., p. 183.
14. Dyson, *Yeats, Eliot and R. S. Thomas*, p. 310.
15. In *The Way of It*, poems by R. S. Thomas, drawings by Barry Hirst (Sunderland: Ceolfrith Press, 1977) p. 20.
16. Ibid., p. 19.
17. Ibid., p. 6.

NOTES TO CHAPTER 8: GOD'S DIALECT

1. In *Later Poems, 1972–1982*. All verse quotations in this chapter are from this collection unless otherwise indicated.
2. In *Frequencies* (London: Macmillan, 1978) p. 11.
3. Ibid., p. 49.
4. Simone Weil, *Lectures on Philosophy*, trs. H. S. Price, introduction by Peter Winch (Cambridge: Cambridge University Press, 1978) pp. 171–2.
5. Merchant, *R. S. Thomas*, p. 97.
6. In *Frequencies*, p. 16.
7. A. M. Allchin, 'Emerging: a Look at Some of R. S. Thomas' More Recent Poems', *Poetry Wales*, Spring 1972, p. 120.
8. In *Frequencies*, p. 34.
9. Ibid., pp. 26–7.
10. Merchant, *R. S. Thomas*, p. 97.
11. Ibid., p. 98.
12. Allen Tate, 'The Symbolic Imagination', in *Essays of Four Decades* (London: Oxford University Press, 1970) p. 431. Quoted in 'A Frame for Poetry', *Times Literary Supplement*, 3 Mar 1966.
13. J. R. Jones, 'Love as Perception of Meaning', in *Religion and Understanding*, ed. D. Z. Phillips (Oxford: Basil Blackwell, 1967) p. 149.
14. Ibid., p. 150.
15. Ibid.
16. Ibid., p. 151.

NOTES TO CHAPTER 9: BETWIXT AND BETWEEN

1. Wallace Stevens, 'Sunday Morning', in *Selected Poems* (London: Faber and Faber, 1953) p. 30.
2. In *Later Poems 1972–1982*. All verse quotations in this chapter are from this collection unless otherwise indicated.
3. Kierkegaard, *Purity of Heart*, pp. 176–7.

4. In *Between Here and Now* (London: Macmillan, 1981) p. 15.
5. Ibid., p. 39.
6. Ibid., p. 59.
7. Ibid., p. 41.
8. Ibid., p. 45.
9. Ibid., p. 19.
10. Ibid., p. 65.
11. Ibid., p. 71.
12. Ibid., p. 101.
13. Norman Malcolm, 'The Relation of Language to Instinctive Behaviour', *Philosophical Investigations*, V, no. 1 (Jan 1982).
14. Ludwig Wittgenstein, *On Certainty*, trs. D. Paul and G. E. M. Anscombe (Oxford: Basil Blackwell, 1969) p. 475.
15. Malcolm, in *Philosophical Investigations*, V, no. 1 p. 3.
16. Ibid.
17. Ibid., p. 5.
18. Ibid., pp. 5–6.
19. Ludwig Wittgenstein, 'Cause and Effect: Intuitive Awareness', *Philosophia*, VI, nos 3–4 (Sep–Dec 1976), selected and ed. Rush Rhees, trs. Peter Winch, p. 416.
20. Ludwig Wittgenstein, *Culture and Value*, trs. Peter Winch (Oxford: Basil Blackwell, 1980) p. 31
21. Weil, *Lectures on Philosophy*, p. 51.
22. Ludwig Wittgenstein, *The Blue and Brown Books* (Oxford: Basil Blackwell, 1958) p. 24.
23. Weil, *Lectures on Philosophy*, p. 31; Peter Winch, Introduction, ibid., p. 12.

NOTES TO CHAPTER 10: A SACRIFICE OF LANGUAGE?

1. In *Song at the Year's Turning*, p. 27.
2. In *Later Poems 1972–1982*. All verse quotations in this chapter are from this collection.
3. R. S. Thomas, 'A Frame for Poetry', *Times Literary Supplement*, 3 Mar 1966, p. 169.
4. Ibid., p. 169.
5. I have benefited from a discussion of this poem with George Evans.
6. See Brian Morris, 'The Topography of R. S. Thomas', in *Critical Writings on R. S. Thomas*, p. 152.
7. *The Penguin Book of Religious Verse*, p. 11.

R. S. Thomas: Selective Biography and Bibliography

1913   Born in Cardiff.

1935   Graduated in the University of Wales. Read Latin at the University College of North Wales, Bangor.

1937   Ordained in the Church in Wales.

1942   Rector of the parish of Manafon in Montgomeryshire (Powys).

1946   *The Stones of the Field* (Carmarthen: Druid Press). Containing 37 poems. Thomas's first volume.

1952   *An Acre of Land* (Newtown: Montgomeryshire Printing Co.). Containing 30 new poems.

1953   *The Minister* (Newton: Montgomeryshire Printing Co.). A poem for four voices first broadcast in the BBC Welsh Home Service on Thursday, 18 Sep 1952.

1954   Vicar of St Michael's, Eglwys Fach, Dyfed.

1955   *Song at the Year's Turning: Poems 1942–1954* (London: Rupert Hart-Davis). Selections from the previous three volumes and 19 new poems.

1958   *Poetry for Supper* (London: Rupert Hart-Davis). 36 new poems.

1959   Heinemann Award of the Royal Society of Literature.

1961   *Tares* (London: Rupert Hart-Davis). 36 new poems.

1963   *The Bread of Truth* (London: Rupert Hart-Davis). 39 new poems.

1964   Queen's Gold Medal for Poetry.

1966   *Pietà* (London: Rupert Hart-Davis). 35 new poems.

1967   Vicar of Eglwys Hywyn Sant, Aberdaron, on the tip of the Llŷn Peninsula.

1968   *Not that he Brought Flowers* (London: Rupert Hart-Davis). 37 new poems.
        Welsh Arts Council Major Prize for contribution to the literature of Wales.

1972   *H'm* (London: Macmillan). 37 new poems.
        Young and Old (London: Chatto and Windus). 28 new poems ostensibly written for children.

1973   *Selected Poems 1946–1968* (London: Rupert Hart-Davis). 86 poems selected from his first 22 years of publication.

1974   *What is a Welshman?* (Llandybie: Christopher Davies). 12 new poems.
1975   *Laboratories of the Spirit* (London: Macmillan). 60 new poems.
1976   *Abercuawg* (Llandysul: Gomer Press). Literature Address at Royal National Eisteddfod, Cardigan.
1977   *The Way Of It* (Sunderland: Ceolfrith.Press). 18 new poems and 12 drawings by Barry Hirst.
1978   *Frequencies* (London: Macmillan). 42 new poems.
Retires to Porth Neigwl, near Aberdaron.
1981   *Between Here and Now* (London: Macmillan). 63 new poems.
1983   *Later Poems 1972–1982* (London: Macmillan). A selection of 123 poems from 1972 volumes onwards and 43 new poems.

Bibliography

A. R. S. THOMAS: PROSE WORKS CITED IN THE TEXT

The Penguin Book of Religious Verse, ed. with an introduction by R. S. Thomas (Harmondsworth: Penguin, 1963).
Selected Poems of Edward Thomas, selected with an introduction by R. S. Thomas (London: Faber and Faber, 1964).
R. S. Thomas, 'A Frame for Poetry', *Times Literary Supplement*, 3 Mar 1966.
A Choice of George Herbert's Verse, selected with an introduction by R. S. Thomas (London: Faber and Faber, 1967).
'R. S. Thomas: Priest and Poet', transcript of John Ormond's film for BBC television, broadcast on 2 Apr 1972, in *Poetry Wales*, Spring 1972.
R. S. Thomas Selected Prose, ed. Sandra Anstey, introduction by Ned Thomas (Bridgend: Poetry of Wales Press, 1983).

B. WORKS ON R. S. THOMAS CITED IN THE TEXT

Ackerman, John, 'Man and Nature in the Poetry of R. S. Thomas', *Poetry Wales*, Spring 1972.
Adams, Sam, 'A Note on Four Poems', ibid.
Allchin, A. M., 'Emerging: A Look at Some of R. S. Thomas' More Recent Poems', ibid.
Conran, Anthony, 'R. S. Thomas and the Anglo-Welsh Crisis', ibid.
Davies, James A., 'Participating Readers: Three Poems by R. S. Thomas', *Poetry Wales*, XVIII, no. 4 (1983).
Dyson, A. E., *Yeats, Eliot and R. S. Thomas* (London: Macmillan, 1981).
Jenkins, Randal, 'R. S. Thomas: Occasional Prose', in *Critical Writings on R. S. Thomas*, ed. Sandra Anstey (Bridgend: Poetry of Wales Press, 1982).
Mathias, Roland, 'Philosophy and Religion in the Poetry of R. S. Thomas', *Poetry Wales*, Spring 1972.
Merchant, W. Moelwyn, *R. S. Thomas*, Writers of Wales (Cardiff: University of Wales Press, 1979).

Mole, John, 'Signals from the Periphery', in *Critical Writings on R. S. Thomas*, ed. Sandra Anstey (Bridgend: Poetry of Wales Press, 1982).
Morris, Brian, 'The Topography of R. S. Thomas', ibid.
Nightingale, Benedict, 'Hewer of Verses', ibid.
Phillips, D. Z., 'Seeking the Poem in the Pain', in *Through a Darkening Glass* (Indiana: University of Notre Dame Press; and Oxford: Basil Blackwell, 1982).
Thomas, R. George, Review of *H'm*, in *Poetry Wales*, Spring 1972.
Wilson, Timothy, 'R. S. Thomas', in *Critical Writings on R. S. Thomas*, ed. Sandra Anstey (Bridgend: Poetry of Wales Press, 1982).

C. OTHER WORKS CITED IN THE TEXT

Drury, M. O'C., 'Some Notes on Conversations with Wittgenstein', in *Ludwig Wittgenstein – Personal Recollections*, ed. Rush Rhees (Oxford: Basil Blackwell, 1981).
Eliot, T. S., *The Idea of a Christian Society* (London: Faber and Faber, 1982).
Freud, Sigmund, *The Future of an Illusion* (London: Hogarth Press, 1962).
Hume, David, *Dialogues Concerning Natural Religion*, ed. N. Kemp-Smith (Chicago: Bobbs-Merrill).
Jones, J. R., 'Love as a Perception of Meaning', in *Religion and Understanding*, ed. D. Z. Phillips (Oxford: Basil Blackwell, 1967).
Keats, John, 'Ode on a Grecian Urn', in *Keats: Poetical Works* (London: Oxford University Press, 1970).
Kierkegaard, Søren, *Purity of Heart*, trs. Douglas Steere (New York: Harper Torchbooks, 1956).
Malcolm, Norman, 'The Relation of Language to Instinctive Behaviour', *Philosophical Investigations*, V, no. 1 (Jan 1982).
O'Connor, Flannery, *A Good Man is Hard to Find* (London: Faber and Faber, 1968).
———, *Mystery and Manners*, selected and ed. Sally and Robert Fitzgerald (New York: Farrar, Straus and Giroux,1969).
Phillips, D. Z., 'Knowledge, Patience and Faust' and 'Meaning, Memory and Longing' in *Through a Darkening Glass* (Indiana: University of Notre Dame Press; and Oxford: Basil Blackwell, 1982).
———, *The Concept of Prayer* (1965; Oxford: Basil Blackwell, 1981).
Stevens, Wallace, 'Sunday Morning', in *Selected Poems* (London: Faber and Faber, 1953).
Tate, Allen, 'The Symbolic Imagination', in *Essays of Four Decades* (London: Oxford University Press, 1970).
Weil, Simone, 'Draft for a Statement of Human Obligations', in *Selected*

Essays, trs. Richard Rees (London: Oxford University Press, 1962).
_____, *First and Last Notebooks* (London: Oxford University Press, 1970).
_____, *Lectures on Philosophy*, trs. H. S. Price (Cambridge: Cambridge University Press, 1978).
_____, *Waiting on God*, trs. Emma Craufurd (London: Fontana, 1959).
Winch, Peter, 'Can a Good Man Be Harmed?', in *Ethics and Action* (London: Routledge and Kegan Paul, 1972).
_____, Introduction to Simone Weil, *Lectures on Philosophy*, trs. H. S. Price (Cambridge: Cambridge University Press, 1978).
Wittgenstein, Ludwig, *The Blue and the Brown Books* (Oxford: Basil Blackwell, 1958).
_____, *On Certainty*, trs. D. Paul and G. E. M. Anscombe (Oxford: Basil Blackwell, 1969).
_____, *Culture and Value*, trs. Peter Winch (Oxford: Basil Blackwell, 1980).
_____, 'Cause and Effect: Intuitive Awareness', selected and ed. Rush Rhees, trs. Peter Winch, *Philosophia*, VI, nos 3–4 (Sep–Dec 1976).

Index

185